CW01024286

Causation

Key Concepts in Philosophy
Joseph Keim Campbell, *Free Will*
Roy T. Cook, *Paradoxes*
Douglas Edwards, *Properties*
Ian Evans and Nicolas D. Smith, *Knowledge*

Causation

Douglas Kutach

polity

First published in 2014 by Polity Press

Polity Press
65 Bridge Street
Cambridge CB2 1UR, UK

Polity Press
350 Main Street
Malden, MA 02148, USA

ISBN-13: 978-0-7456-5995-4
ISBN-13: 978-0-7456-5996-1(pb)

A catalogue record for this book is available from the British Library.

Typeset in 10.5 on 12 pt Sabon
by Toppan Best-set Premedia Limited
Printed and bound in Great Britain by T.J. International, Padstow, Cornwall

The publisher has used its best endeavours to ensure that the URLs for external websites referred to in this book are correct and active at the time of going to press. However, the publisher has no responsibility for the websites and can make no guarantee that a site will remain live or that the content is or will remain appropriate.

Every effort has been made to trace all copyright holders, but if any have been inadvertently overlooked the publisher will be pleased to include any necessary credits in any subsequent reprint or edition.

For further information on Polity, visit our website: www.politybooks.com

Contents

1
Introduction: All Things Causal

At the beginning of every course I teach on causation, I like to mention three reasons for studying causation. First, it is the most important relation in the universe. As the great philosopher once said, "It surrounds us and penetrates us. It binds the galaxy together." Second, virtually every other topic you can study depends on causation: science, history, music, business, law, medicine, and most important of all, bicycle repair.

My third reason is difficult for me to communicate without injecting some philosophical jargon, so I will leave you hanging for a while. In the meantime, you should think about reasons for yourself. Before, during, and after reading every chapter, ask yourself, "Why is causation worth studying? What is there to learn from philosophers musing about cause and effect? Is there any conclusion that could transform my conception of reality?" I can intimate to you that by spending a bit of time mulling over such questions, I have struck upon an idea that has altered my opinion about virtually everything I care about and everything I do. I hope that by introducing you to some tools for investigating causation, you will be encouraged to revolutionize your own conception of reality. If you succeed, please track me down and let me know. I would love to hear about it. We humans don't keep in touch enough.

It's going to take a modicum of effort for us to sort out what causation is and how to define it. We all have some basic ability to apply terms like 'cause' and 'effect', so we can start out by assuming that 'causation' is just another name for the relation between cause and effect, whatever that turns out to be. We will see soon enough that it is problematic to decipher expressions like 'it causes' and 'it is a cause of', but on the bright side, that is a sign that it's an ideal topic for drawing the sorts of distinctions that are the hallmark of good philosophy.

Before digging into details, you should be aware of the scope of a philosophical investigation of causation. Philosophy, it has been said, is in the business of understanding "how things in the broadest possible sense of the term hang together in the broadest possible sense of the term."[1] My goal is to help you to learn how philosophers have tried to understand causation insofar as it applies generally to all things. That means the focus of discussion is not on how we humans acquire our causal concepts, nor on how scientists discover causes, nor on how various historical figures have thought about causation. Instead, the goal is for you to acquaint yourself with a map of the contemporary conceptual landscape. We will be trying to answer questions like, "Which ways of thinking about causation are fruitful?" "What obstacles have been overcome in understanding causation?" and "What are the outstanding deficiencies in our current theories of causation?"

In this first chapter, I will avoid introducing any theories. Instead, I will highlight four distinctions that I have personally found to be insightful and helpful for organizing all of the information to come.

- singular vs. general causation
- linear vs. non-linear interaction
- productive vs. difference-making causation
- influence-based vs. pattern-based causation

I will now proceed through a discussion of each distinction.

Singular vs. General Causation

A singular event is a particular occurrence in the history of the universe. It can be identified in terms of its location in time and space, and it can be described in terms of the properties and relations it instantiates. When discussing singular causation, we typically designate one singular event as the effect. We then consider all the singular events that count as partial causes of that one effect. Philosophers use the term 'cause' for what is more accurately described as a partial cause. **Singular causation** is the relation that holds between any single effect and each one of its singular (partial) causes. We often express claims of singular causation in the past tense: "*c* was one of the causes of *e*," or "*c* caused *e*," because singular causation is usually evaluated in retrospect.

A general event is a type of event. By their nature, event types can be instantiated in multiple locations in space and time, and they can be described in terms of whatever properties and relations constitute that sort of event. We often express claims of general causation in the present tense: "*C* causes *E*," or "*C*s cause *E*s." **General causation** is the relation that holds between an event type *E* and any event type *C* that tends to cause (or bring about) *E*.

(I like to use lowercase letters for singular causes and uppercase letters for general causes.)

To acquire an intuitive feel for the difference between singular causation and general causation, consider the encouraging tale of Hobo, the scruffy hound. Hobo was generously helping to reduce food waste around dumpsters in Moore, Oklahoma, when she was suddenly cornered by the resident dogcatcher. I happen to know this guy personally, and trust me, you do not want him to catch you whether you are a dog or not. Fortunately, Moore is situated in a tornado corridor, and at the very moment when Hobo had abandoned all hope of escape, a tornado touched down and hoisted Hobo high into the air, carrying her over to nearby Kitchen Lake, where she splashed down and swam to shore uninjured. Having learned a valuable lesson, Hobo migrated eastward, last anyone has heard.

In the particular fragment of history described by this very true story, Hobo was rescued by the tornado. The tornado was a major cause of Hobo's survival because dogs snared by the dogcatcher tend not to last long. More formally, we stipulate that the event of interest to us (playing the role of effect) is the dog's survival for several more years. Examining what happened in the fragment of history encompassing Hobo's narrow escape, we can rightly declare that the tornado's lifting of Hobo was one of the causes of her survival. In general, however, tornados do not cause dogs to survive for a long time; they pose a mortal danger. So, the tornado was a *singular* cause of survival even though tornados are not a *general* cause of survival.

Let's now engage in some philosophy by examining the distinction.

1. Note that in the definitions I offered for singular and general causation (marked in boldface), I used the term 'cause' on both sides. Therefore, I have not defined causation in terms of something non-causal. In philosophical jargon, I have not provided a *reductive* definition of causation. So far, I have merely attempted to distinguish the conceptual role of singular and general causes enough to convey what makes them different from each other, not to specify what each is in full detail.

2. Ordinary language carries connotations that some partial causes are more noteworthy than others, and much of the phrasing used for expressing claims of causation can obscure what is at stake in disputes over causation.

- One can distinguish between background and foreground causes: The last straw you placed on the camel caused its back injury. We think of the presence of the last straw as being especially prominent and thus figuratively in the foreground even though the last straw was no heavier than each of the previous thousands of straws, which we think of as in the background.
- One can distinguish proximal (or proximate) causes from distal causes. The proximal causes are nearby in space and time and the distal causes are far away in space or time. For example, we say "Julius Caesar's death was caused by assassins," not that his death was caused by his own birth. Yet, upon reflection, it becomes evident that Caesar's birth set off a causal chain that led inexorably to his demise.
- One can distinguish enabling causes from activating causes. We say that what caused the blaze was the cow's having kicked over the lamp. We do not say that

the presence of the many wooden buildings tightly packed together *caused* the fire. A more perspicuous description would indicate that the density of wooden structures caused the blaze to engulf most of the city by enabling the fire to spread and that the toppled lamp was an activating or triggering cause.

In all three examples, we have a tendency to deny the status of cause to the background, distal, and enabling causes, even though when we examine our reasons for doing so, we find that objectively they have the same status as events we are happy to designate as causes. In such cases, the features that distinguish them from *genuine* causes appear to be merely pragmatic. The partial causes we identify as non-causes might be less important to us, or they might be less amenable to our manipulations, or they might be so pervasive that it would be misleading to draw attention to them.

When philosophers discuss causation, they usually seek (or at least claim to seek) an egalitarian[2] conception of causation that strives to count the background and distal and enabling causes as bona fide causes. They bracket the goal of evaluating which causes are more important and the task of ascertaining whether one of the causes deserves to be designated as *the* cause.

The subtleties of language and the general culture, however, allow these observations to be easily overlooked. For example, an expression of the form 'a cause of *e*' might be construed as more or less equivalent to 'one of the causes of *e*', but it might also be understood as 'something that caused *e*'. If these two renderings of 'a cause' sound like they say the same thing, imagine a scenario where someone buys a winning lottery ticket. Is Jennifer's purchase of a lottery ticket *a cause* of her receiving money from the lottery agency? The purchase in this case was certainly *one of the causes* because she had to play to win, but the purchase was not *something that caused* her to win because it gave her only a one in a million chance. If we identify *e*'s singular causes by answering, "Which events *caused e?*" we might arrive at different events than by answering, "Which events were *among the causes* of *e?*" The first question is usually answered by citing the events that were the most important contributing causes to *e* at the time they occurred. The second question is usually answered by citing events that somehow played a positive role in the overall development toward the occurrence of *e*. Philosophers are almost always concerned with the egalitarian conception of cause that corresponds to the second question.

3. Our linguistic idioms can also mislead us about causation to the extent that we do not separate out logical or definitional connections among events. For example, if someone answers the question, "How did Julius Caesar die?" by noting that he was assassinated, that conveys relevant information about the events that caused his death. However, it is somewhat misleading to say, "The assassination of Caesar was a cause of Caesar's death," because assassination implies by definition a corresponding death. The definitional link is not a constituent of the causal connections among the conspirators and Caesar, and we need to ignore it when ascertaining causes.

Such definitional linkages are not rare because the term 'cause' is itself loaded. When we describe an event *c* as 'one of the causes of *e*', that presupposes that *e* occurred. Nothing can be a cause of an event that does not occur. So, when investigating what aspect of the cause makes its effect occur, we need to ignore the fact that *its being one of the causes* ensures the occurrence of its effect by definition. We do this simply by not treating "is a cause of *e*" as if it describes a property of *c* that can play a role in causation.

4. An alternative way to express the distinction between singular and general causes is to say that particular instances of causation are cases of **token causation** and that causal generalities concern **type causation**. The difference between types and tokens is meant to be widely applicable, not just to events. For example, the typographic character that comes first in alphabetic order is a *type*, which we sometimes call "the letter A" or just "A." Here are five of its tokens:

A a A *a a*

When we say that the line of text contains only one letter, we are saying that there is only one letter-type instantiated. When we say that the line of text contains exactly five letters, we are saying that there are five tokens of this one letter-type.

Applying the type–token distinction to causation, we say that the generality that holds from smoking to lung cancer is type causation (or type-level causation) and that any particular instance of lung cancer that was caused by smoking is token causation.

Is there any reason to speak of singular vs. general causation rather than token vs. type causation? They are mostly the same distinction, but perhaps the following example highlights a nuance. We nowadays take for granted that unicorns have never existed,[3] yet it seems reasonable to assert that if there had been any unicorns that walked in mud, they would have caused hoof-shaped impressions in the mud. One way to describe this possibility is to say that there is type causation between unicorns stepping in mud and the existence of hoof-marks. This type causation has no tokens because there never have been any real unicorns. On the one hand, it seems reasonable to speak of type-level causal relations among unicorn-events just because unicorns are a subtype of hoofed animal. Hoofed animals in general cause hoof-marks, and more specific hoofed species like unicorns will generally cause hoof-marks when present in muddy environments. On the other hand, when we speak of causal generalities we tend to have in mind cases where there is a repeatedly instantiated pattern of singular causation. Many individual horses have walked in mud and thereby caused hoof-marks, but no instance of a unicorn having caused a hoof-mark exists. So, perhaps we could let the term "general causation" refer to type causation that has corresponding tokens in the actual world, and make clear that "type causation" does not require that the causal regularity ever be realized.

Just to add some redundancy, philosophers have recently begun to adopt a distinction between **actual causation** and **potential causation**. As far as I can tell, 'actual cause' means the same thing as 'token cause' and the same thing as 'singular cause'.[4] Potential causation, I think, is meant to encompass causal relations that involve unicorns in addition to causal relations among existing entities.

5. Finally, most philosophical work on causation concentrates on singular causation, and there appears to be a prevailing opinion that if an adequate account of singular causes could ever be found, it would be relatively easy to construct

a complementary account of general causation. The idea, perhaps, is that if we have a good rule telling us whether one chosen event is a cause of our given effect – using information about its surroundings, any operative laws, and perhaps other parameters – then that same rule will automatically identify the full collection of causes. One reason to suspect that the connection between singular and general causation is more subtle is that on the few occasions where rules for deriving general from singular causation have been specified, there has been a curious lack of detail.[5]

More important, there appears to be a consensus among experts that a satisfactory account of general causation cannot be provided without incorporating an account of singular causation. The worry perhaps is that a generality like "inhaling the fumes from modeling glue causes headaches" cannot hold unless there are objective enough facts about whether particular inhalations have caused particular headaches. Unlike unicorns, the causes here are not fictional.

Let's sum it all up. The main distinction so far has been laid out in terms of several terminological choices: *singular vs. general* causation, *token vs. type* causation, and *actual vs. potential* causation. These are basically the same. Along the way, we also noted that the sort of singular causation philosophers care about is *egalitarian*.

Linear vs. Non-Linear Interaction

Think about a spring-operated scale used to measure weights. On an empty scale, you place a 1 kg mass and the scale moves down 1 cm. Then, you place a 3 kg mass on the scale and it moves down 3 cm more. What is causally responsible for the current position of the scale? Uncontroversially, the placement of a total of 4 kg on the scale caused it to move 4 cm. But are both weights equally causes?

In one sense, they are. Without the smaller mass, the scale would not stretch to 4 cm. Also, without the larger mass, the scale would not stretch to 4 cm. Both masses are needed for the observed effect. We call this a case of **joint causation**. The two masses jointly cause the 4 cm displacement of the scale.

In another sense, they are unequal. The larger mass is responsible for three-fourths of the displacement. It is pulling down three times as much as the smaller mass.

Insofar as we are seeking egalitarian causes, the two placements of the masses are equally causes. And insofar as we are making predictions or explanations, we can use unequal quantities to represent the relative strength of the causes. The effect is proportional to the relative strength of its causes, and in the language of mathematics, we say that the effect here is a linear function of the two causes.

Is there some problem here? As far as I can tell, there isn't, but there are non-linear causal relationships as well, which we need to consider. A good example of non-linear causation is when an effect is generated by passing some sort of threshold.

Suppose you place 70 separate 1 kg masses on the scale at once, and the scale breaks, because it holds at most 50 kg. What were the causes of the scale's breaking? It seems reasonable at first to say that the entire collection of masses (being on the scale at once) caused the breakage. But what about other causes? In particular, can we ascertain whether each individual mass was a (partial) cause of the breakage?

On the one hand, we can say that no individual mass made a significant difference. If any one of the 70 had been omitted, the scale would still have broken. On the other hand, we know that all 70 together broke the scale and that they all weigh exactly the same. That suggests we should apply the principle that if some of them are responsible for the breakage, so are all the others. In that case, each mass is one of the causes of the scale breaking.

Unlike the previous linear case, there is a potential problem here for the egalitarian conception of causation. We have two lines of reasoning appealing to the equality of causes and drawing opposite conclusions. One says that because none of the individuals caused the breakage, none of them were causes. The other says that some of the single masses had to be causes of the breakage, so they were all causes. The problem is that attributing the status of 'cause' (in the egalitarian sense) is a binary matter. Every event is either "one of the causes" or it isn't. The framework philosophers operate under does not allow us to identify the placement of each single mass as one-seventieth of a cause or one-fiftieth of a cause or any other fraction.

One common response to such examples is to point out that some cases of causation involve **overdetermination**. Placing two 100 kg masses on the scale causes breakage. Because each of them alone was enough to ensure breakage and because they are identical in all relevant respects, both masses are individually culpable for the breakage. We say that these two causes overdetermined that the scale broke. No problem here.

One can now attempt to impose the same reasoning on the scenario where the breakage was caused by the 70 small masses. We can motivate attributing causal blame to each individual mass by noting that in exemplary cases of overdetermination, an event can be a cause even though it was entirely redundant. So it is no requirement for causation that if the cause had not been there, the effect would not have occurred. Furthermore, because the full complement of 70 masses caused the breakage, each of the masses being on the scale was individually and equally a *partial* cause of the breakage. Finally, to say that some event c was a partial cause of e is (in philosophers' parlance) the same as saying that c is one of the causes of e.

I personally find that this way of imposing the framework of egalitarian causes is acceptable as far as it goes, but it can go too far by identifying so many events as causes that most of the causal distinctions we want to draw will need to be cashed out in terms of some further theory that assesses the relative importance of the many egalitarian causes.

If we have settled on the goal of seeking a theory of causation under which every event is designated either as a partial cause of e or as a non-cause of e without any allowing for degrees of causation, then presumably we are going to simplify (in our modeling activity) some aspects of nature's causal structure. The philosopher's hope is that this simplification is not an oversimplification.

To what extent the egalitarian simplification misleads rather than leads, however, is an issue you should allow to nag you continually. You ought to wake up in the middle of the night startled and ask yourself, "Why is everyone arguing about this egalitarian conception of singular causation? What is it good for?"

Productive vs. Difference-Making Causation

It is important not to let the discussion spin out of control by becoming too abstract. Let us turn at once to a social scenario incorporating the non-linear causation we just discussed. The purpose of the following example is to illustrate two points. (1) In many cases we care about, causal responsibility should not in general be distributed among multiple causes in terms of a *fraction of responsibility*. (2) We sometimes have significantly different conceptions of causation driving our judgments of causal responsibility. In particular, I want to point out that we sometimes think of a cause as somehow generating or producing its effect, and at other times we think of a cause as something that makes a difference as to whether or how its effect comes about. It is not currently well known whether (and how) these two conceptions are compatible.

Once upon a time, there were two nearby islands. Paul was the lone inhabitant of one island, and he had a small boat for fishing. Vivian was the lone inhabitant of the other island, which hosted abundant stringy plants that she harvested for rope fiber. By working alone, each collected enough food for his or her own survival, but just barely and with several periods of hunger. By cooperating, however, they could gather enough food to be healthy year-round and to preserve some leftovers for insurance.

Vivian had already spent an enormous amount of time making a few large nets out of plant fiber. She haggled with Paul, who agreed to let her use his boat if she gave him half of the fish. She acceded and gathered heaps of fish from the deeper waters. Before handing any fish over, Vivian reconsidered the fairness of dividing the fish equally between her and Paul. Vivian suggested to Paul that it was not fair for him to take half of the fish because he did not do any work; he just let her use the boat. But Paul pointed out that without his boat, she wouldn't have gotten the huge stock of fish. Using his boat made all the difference between going hungry and having a huge stockpile. Vivian then noted that the same observation applied to her. Without the net, she could not have caught so many fish.

There are two conflicting arguments here concerning how to divide the cooperative surplus fairly. Vivian, we might say, was suggesting that the rights to the fish are earned by doing work and that the surplus should be distributed proportional to the amount of labor expended. Paul was countering that they are both free agents and if they both agree to a deal, what is fair is to stick to the terms: "If I hold out until you agree to give me half the fish," Paul continues, "and you accept, it's fair for me to get half. So long as everyone consents, there's nothing more to discuss."

I first learned about this problem of cooperative surplus while studying political philosophy. Vivian's line of argument fits in the tradition of John Locke, who argued that a person has a right to private property if he mixes in his personal labor.[6] Paul's line of argument follows the classic libertarian tradition by saying, "What everyone freely agrees to is fair."

I later realized that debates about fairness (and other ethical issues) share important features with debates about causation. The main similarity I want to point out is the non-linear causal relationship between the activities of Vivian and Paul and the total resulting amount of fish.

Let's first consider the case of a linear relationship between effort and result. When they were working alone on their own islands and their fishing conditions were equal, it might have been reasonable (at least as a crude approximation) to declare that a fair allotment of fish should have been proportional to the fraction each catches or perhaps to the fraction of work each does. If Paul chooses to work twice as long as Vivian and he catches twice as many fish, he should get his two-thirds of the total. Similarly with regard to causation, when a scale is stretched by holding a 1 kg and a 2 kg block, the 2 kg mass is responsible for two-thirds of the stretching. Furthermore, we can state these relations in terms of difference-making. We can reasonably conclude (because they are working by themselves) that if Paul had chosen not to fish at all, then Vivian would have still caught the same amount. So, Paul's actual amount of fishing activity is responsible for their having a combined catch that would have been two-thirds smaller without his effort.

For contrast, let us now consider the non-linear relationship between effort and result that exists in the original scenario. If Paul had chosen not to let his boat be used, he and Vivian would each have caught only a small amount of fish, say 1 kg each. By their working together, a total of 100 kg was caught. So, the extra amount of fish that was gathered because of Paul's letting Vivian use his boat is 99 kg. Similarly, the extra amount of fish that was gathered because Vivian constructed her nets is 99 kg. In this sense, each person individually made a 99 percent difference in the amount of fish caught. This is the problem of cooperative surplus: that it is impossible for both of them to get 99 percent of the fish.

When stuck in such a situation, one answer is to accept that both people made the same 99 percent difference in the amount of fish and split the bounty equally. That is Paul's bargaining position. Another answer is to incorporate other factors such as the amount of time and energy spent in active retrieval of the fish. Vivian argued that because Paul did not engage actively in collecting the fish, he does not deserve an equal share even if he was successful at bargaining for it.

What we have in Vivian and Paul's arguments is a divide between looking at how much difference each made to the effect and looking at how much energy or effort was expended. Vivian sees herself as more responsible for the catch because she exerted more effort and engaged in more production. Paul sees himself as equally responsible for the catch because he made just as much of a difference.

This distinction applies generally to theories of causation. Some treatments emphasize that causation is *productive*. Causes *make* their effects happen. Causes *bring about* their effects. Causes *give rise to* their effects. Causes *alter* and *change* the world. Other accounts emphasize that causation *affects*. Causes are *difference-makers*. Without the cause, the effect *would not have* happened. Causation is recognized by *intervening* in the world and *manipulating* causes.

This divide between a productive conception of causation and a difference-making conception will play a significant organizational role in the rest of our discussion of causation, but for now I just want to suggest that one reason there are many difficult decisions to make about how to distribute the goods of society fairly is that the goods come to us by way of non-linear causality. The simple idea that we should proportion reward for good outcomes and punishments for bad outcomes by the amount each cause contributed to the effect runs smack into the problem that in most cases, there is no objective way to proportion causal responsibility. Typically, an effect has a complicated tangle of causal relationships, and we search in vain for a formula for the *degree* to which one cause is more important than the other. It is a useful exercise to mull over the range of issues in our society that exhibit non-linearity owing to the underlying causal relations being non-linear.

Influence-Based vs. Pattern-Based Causation

I think the most underappreciated distinction in the history of philosophical musings on the subject of causation appears in Michael Dummett's (1964) article entitled "Bringing about the Past." In this paper, Dummett attacks a stock argument against the possibility of influencing the past, namely the argument that "you cannot *change* the past; if a thing has happened, it has happened, and you cannot make it not to have happened." He points out that this argument follows the same pattern as the fallacious argument that you cannot affect the future because there is only one way things are eventually going to turn out. Dummett agrees with the widely held view that we should not deny our ability to influence the future just because a single determinate future will eventually occur. But, then, by parity of reasoning, he draws the unorthodox conclusion that we should not dismiss the possibility of influencing the past. He thinks the stock argument – that we cannot affect the past because it has already happened – is just as bad as the argument that we cannot affect the future because it will eventually happen.

The possibility of influencing the past is a fascinating topic, and there are nuances galore to be uncovered. But, because space is short, I will just point out one extraordinarily powerful but only briefly discussed idea in Dummett's article. Here is a quotation from very near the beginning:

> I think that this asymmetry [of causation being directed always toward the future and never toward the past] would reveal itself to us even if we were not *agents* but mere *observers*. It is indeed true, I believe, that our concept of cause is bound up with our concept of intentional action: if an event is properly said to cause the occurrence of a subsequent or simultaneous event, I think it necessarily follows that, if we can find any way of bringing about the former event (in particular, if it is itself a voluntary human action), then it must make sense to speak of bringing it about *in order* that the subsequent event should occur. Moreover, I believe that this connection between something's being a cause and the possibility of using it in order to bring about its effect plays an essential role in the fundamental account of how we ever come to accept causal laws: that is, that we could arrive at any causal beliefs only by beginning with those in which the cause is a voluntary action of ours. Nevertheless, I am inclined to think that we could have some kind of concept of cause, although one differing from that we now have, even if we were mere observers and not agents at all – a kind of intelligent tree. And I also think that even in this case the asymmetry of cause with respect to temporal direction would reveal itself to us.

Here is how I would focus and expand Dummett's position: It proves useful to break up our common but contested conception of causation into two more precise conceptions of causation. Let us say that an **influence-based** conception of causation is one that incorporates some component related to influence or agency or manipulation or intervention. Let us say that a **pattern-based** conception of causation concerns only the patterns in the tapestry of space-time, which comprises everything that has occurred and will occur throughout the history of the universe. The metaphorical "intelligent tree" can be idealized as having complete information about the entire arrangement of every last subatomic particle in the past, present, and future history of everything, but it does not organize this information in any way that implies one part of the universe is affecting another part.

The intelligent tree might organize its knowledge in terms of regularities. It might notice that every time two rocks collide, their total momentum is conserved. The intelligent tree might also reckon the universe in terms of statistical relationships. It might recognize that a certain valley floods on average one out of every ten years, and that when April is extremely rainy, the valley floods seven out of ten years. The tree would not interpret the extremely rainy April in 1745 as a weather event that *made* a flood occur. Nor would it reason by imagining an alternate history where the valley experienced a dry April in 1745 and conclude that the actually heavy rain of 1745 made all the difference in the actual flooding of the valley.

Most contemporary authors do not specify how their theories fit with this distinction I am drawing between influence-based and pattern-based aspects of causation because, as I said, the distinction is underappreciated. But as we proceed deeper into discussion, it should become clearer how this distinction cross-cuts the distinction between production and difference-making. We will see one manifestation of this distinction in theories of causation based on agency and manipulation as well as in the literature on causal modeling and intervention. In the meantime, it will be instructive to consider whether the theoretical approaches we will encounter treat causation as influence-based or as merely pattern-based.

Questions

Q: What is the difference between causation and causality?

A: I don't know of any. As far as I can tell, it is the same thing. At least, if you are writing anything on this topic, you should assume that your reader is not aware of any previously agreed-upon distinction between 'causation' and 'causality'.

Q: I wasn't getting the difference between the influence–pattern distinction and the difference-making–production distinction. You said they "cross-cut," but what does that mean?

A: I just mean that they do not categorize the set of causation theories in the same way. There's a chart in figure 1.1.

Because we haven't talked about any of these theories yet, we are not in a position to examine why I categorized them this way, but my point is simply that the two distinctions are not two ways of saying the same thing.

One way to distinguish influence-based theories of causation from pattern-based theories of causation is in terms of what kinds of concepts they involve. Imagine you have a chart detailing the entire history of the world. It indicates the location of every object at every time. Ask yourself, with such a chart, would you have enough conceptual resources for the theory in question to make sense? If so, it is a pattern-based theory; otherwise, it is an influence-based theory. An influence-based theory needs to supplement information in the chart with information about what the *laws* are or how one hypothetical alteration to part of the historical tapestry would *affect* other parts.

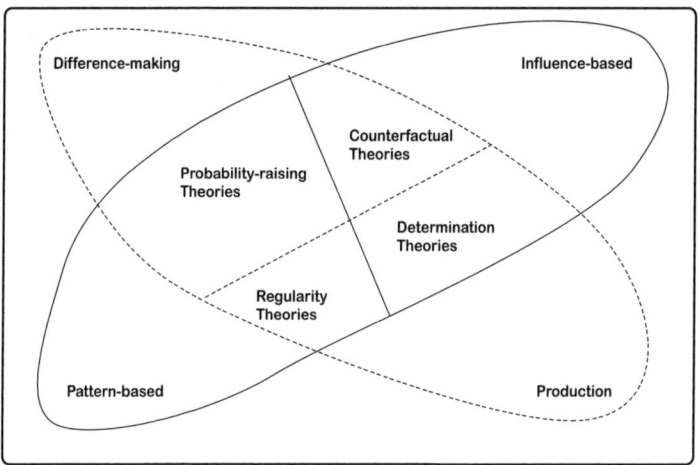

Figure 1.1

One way to think about the distinction between difference-making and production is to attend to whether the theory only requires you to consider what happens in the actual history of the universe, without needing to consider alternate ways history could have developed. Productive theories postulate rules for how a given collection of causes at one time give rise to what happens at other times, whereas difference-making accounts incorporate comparisons between two or more possible arrangements of causes.

I have deliberately drawn figure 1.1 to allow for the possibility that there are other ways of thinking about causation that do not fit these distinctions, but probably the more important point to keep in mind is that this chart provides only a rough map to help maintain a basic level of organization. There are some important regions of overlap that I have oversimplified away, and people can have reasonable disagreements with this way of demarcating the conceptual landscape.

2
Causal Oomph

Philosophy encompasses some subject matter so ridiculously broad that any studious effort to address it should come across as outrageously ambitious. The topic of reality is one of these subjects. **Metaphysics** is the name philosophers use to designate the discipline where one attempts to provide a theory of reality. To provide a metaphysical theory, a metaphysics, is to provide a list of the general kinds of things that exist – substances, relations, sensations, facts, space, etc. – and an account of how they all fit together to constitute a comprehensive basis for everything. Metaphysical theories paint a big picture of reality and ignore almost all of the particular details, no matter how important they are to us humans. Don't read a book on metaphysics to find out whether it is healthier to live by the sea or where to find gold, but you could conceivably find something of value if you are interested in whether time is something objectively real or whether instead it is merely some subjective way we organize our experiences.

One of the hypotheses philosophers have been exploring for millennia is the idea that reality consists mainly of a bunch of particular things that inhabit space and persist through time. The basic idea is that reality includes things like oceans, clay, an Eiffel Tower, avalanches, worms, laughter, and people. These entities can be said to exist somewhere in space and to have some duration through time.

A number of philosophers have made this idea more specific and more audacious by suggesting further that all the particular things in the universe are instances of just a few kinds of matter. Long ago in ancient Greece, for example, a character named Leucippus about whom we know very little and his slightly younger contemporary Democritus, a.k.a. the laughing philosopher, tweaked some existing hypotheses by suggesting that reality consists fundamentally of atoms ricocheting around in an otherwise empty space, the void. According to this doctrine of **atomism**, all the objects of public life – fish, sapphires, shadows, and so on – are ultimately just assemblages of these tiny bits of matter. All the complexity we see around us is reducible to various arrangements of atoms.

Although no one today signs off on the full set of hypotheses advanced by ancient atomists, similar doctrines are currently prevalent in academic philosophy: physicalism and materialism. According to **materialism**, fundamental reality consists entirely of matter, and according to **physicalism**, fundamental reality consists entirely of physical stuff like space, time, particles, forces, electromagnetic fields, superstrings, and other entities you might encounter in a physics class. Physicalism and materialism are largely the same doctrine; both of them deny the existence of ghosts, angels, demons, nirvana, heaven, gods, voodoo, and magic.

We here are not in a good position to examine whether the doctrines of physicalism or materialism are *true*. That topic is way too big! I am mentioning them because they provide a stripped-down but still tolerably realistic model of fundamental reality. They help to clarify what is at stake in debates about whether causation is a fundamental component of reality cementing together the various happenings in our world.

In order to investigate whether causation is a fundamental component of reality, it is handy to contrast two ways the world could be fundamentally. Philosophers often speak of "possible worlds" or just "worlds," and by that, they do not mean planets but instead a complete possible history of the universe. I personally think the most helpful way to think about a possible world is to construe it as a *consistent way fundamental reality could be*, any non-contradictory specification of what exists fundamentally and how these fundamental entities are bound together in a totality.

I think it helps here just to dig into some examples. One possible world – let's call it F – consists of space-time completely filled in with some pattern of electric and magnetic force fields and tiny atomic particles. World F, we may imagine, contains a complete history of how all such microphysical stuff is arranged at any time. Furthermore, F includes what is called a fundamental dynamical law, which is a fundamental law that dictates how the complete state of the universe at one time is related to the complete state at other times. This law might specify a functional relationship, so that if F is in the condition C at one time, it will definitely be in condition $f(C)$ an hour later. Such laws are called deterministic laws. Or the law might instead incorporate fundamental chanciness, specifying a rule whereby if F is in condition C at one time, the probability of its being in state C_1 an hour later is p_1, the probability of its being in condition C_2 is p_2, etc. The upshot is that F is fundamentally just a space-time containing a specific historical pattern of material properties instantiated at every location in space at every time together with this dynamical law that cements all of these states together under some rule of governance.

Because F consists entirely of physical stuff, it is a possible world where physicalism holds true. If we wanted to, we could define another possible world, M, that has all the stuff of F but also incorporates sorcerers and some fundamental laws of magic that govern the spells they cast. M is an example of a possible world where physicalism is false.

For further contrast, we can consider yet another possible world, H, defined to be just like F except with all the fundamental laws stripped out. World H consists of a space-time with the exact same pattern of microphysical stuff as F throughout its entire history, but with no fundamental law governing how happenings at one time are related to happenings at other times. In H, things just happen.

The core question about causation addressed in this chapter is whether the actual world is more like H or more like F.

Advocates for the *F* side think there is some sort of fundamental law or some sort of fundamental causal connection binding all the actual historical events (past, present, and future) together into a complete universe. There is something fundamentally at work that allows stuff to make other stuff occur.

Advocates for the *H* side think the world is fundamentally just a bunch of things that happen at various times and places and that all our talk of causation and laws and chance boils down in the end to a conceptual convenience or a handy fiction that proves cognitively useful owing to the happenstance that the actual historical pattern of events fits some remarkably simple descriptions. Although we often call these remarkably simple descriptions "laws," the big philosophical point is that these descriptions of nature, like all other descriptions, do not restrict what nature can do.

Nowadays it is common to honor the legacy of the philosopher David Hume by calling advocates for the *H* side "Humeans" and advocates for the *F* side "Non-Humeans." To what extent David Hume would have endorsed the Humean position is an interesting question in the history of philosophy that we will have to leave aside.

Non-Humeans think the actual world is more like *F*. They think laws do real work out there in nature. Laws take the present state of the universe and use it to produce or generate the future or at least to constrain how the future can turn out. If the fundamental laws are deterministic, they use the current state of the universe to *make* the future occur in exactly one particular way. If the fundamental laws are chancy, they use the current state of the universe to specify probabilities for some set of ways the future *might* occur. Beyond that, it is mere happenstance which possible future becomes actual.

Humeans disagree, arguing that laws are more like rules we ascribe to patterns retrospectively. A law of nature does not *do* anything. By happenstance, the condition of the universe at multiple times might fit some equation, but there is nothing more to it. The actual world, according to this view, is like a complicated pattern in a carpet. The carpet has all sorts of different colors at different locations, like a black fiber at one location with a red fiber next to it. The black fiber does not force its neighbor to be red. The carpet just *is* that way. Imagine that we can orient the carpet so that as we look at it there are horizontal rows of fibers arranged vertically in a rectangular grid. Then suppose we find a remarkably simple mathematical function that takes as input a complete specification of the arrangement of colors in one row and produces as output a complete specification of the arrangement of colors in the row immediately above it and that in every case matches the actual arrangement of the carpet colors. Members of team *H* would agree that it is remarkable that such a complex pattern in the carpet turns out to fit such a simple rule, but the fact that the colors happen to satisfy an equation does not justify thinking that the colors in one row *made* the colors in another row turn out the way they did. Rules don't *do* anything. Laws do not *do* anything. Equations do not *do* anything. They are all just descriptions.

Summarizing now, the central issue in the debate over the metaphysical status of causation is whether fundamental reality ought to include something beyond the mere pattern of historical occurrences – some sort of causal oomph – so that causes fundamentally *make* their effects happen. The expression "causal oomph" does not have any technical meaning. It is merely a playful catch-all term to designate whatever it is in causal relationships that goes beyond the actual occurrences in the entire history of the universe. Causal oomph is that aspect of a cause that does something to help make its effect come into existence.

The big philosophical question is

When *c* causes *e*, is there something in fundamental reality that *makes e* happen?

This is just the question of whether causal oomph exists.

I have now laid out the basic debate over causal oomph in a framework that I personally find helpful for elucidating the main issue. Let us now turn our attention to a more traditional way of approaching this debate, which invokes a stock theory of how causation can be understood as non-fundamental.

The Regularity View of Causation

The regularity view of causation I will describe in this section is a theory of causation in the Humean tradition based on the principle that there is no causal oomph. Philosophers today mainly like to use the regularity view of causation as a foil, a theory that serves as an example against which they can contrast and motivate their own views. It is difficult to find contemporary advocates of the regularity view, though some famous historical figures, like the physicist Ernst Mach (1883, p. 483), have advocated the basic idea:

> There is no cause nor effect in nature; nature has but an individual existence; nature simply *is*. Recurrence of cases in which *A* is always connected with *B*, that is, like results under like circumstances, that is again, the essence of the connection of cause and effect, exist but in the abstraction which we perform for the purpose of mentally reproducing the facts.

The main purpose of a regularity theory of causation is to identify *which* structures in nature make it reasonable for people to believe in causation even though causation is not a component of fundamental reality. According to the regularity theorist, talk of cause–effect relations serves as a convenient gloss concerning how events in the universe happen to be arranged but does not refer to any sort of fundamental binding agent that cements events together.

Here is a basic formulation of the regularity view presented by Stathis Psillos (2009, p. 131):

> The singular event *c* causes the singular event *e* exactly when these three conditions all hold:
>
> 1. *c* is spatio-temporally contiguous to *e*.
> 2. *c* occurs earlier than *e*.
> 3. Events of type *C* always occur with events of type *E*.

The main point of the first condition is to pair the correct instances of *C* and *E* together. For example, Henry just pressed the button on his toaster and that event, c_h, caused his bread to become toast, e_h. On the other side of the world ten hours later, Katia pressed the button on her toaster and that event, c_k, caused her bread to become toast, e_k. If these are bona fide cases of causation according to the regularity view, toaster activation events, C, always occur with toast creation events, E. But we want to avoid saying that c_h caused e_k because Henry did not toast Katia's bread. The first condition is included to rule this out.

Similarly, the second condition is meant to forbid effects from causing their causes. Suppose there are some (spatio-temporally contiguous) Cs and Es that always co-occur, with each C happening before its corresponding E. Without the second condition, it will turn out that Cs cause Es and also that Es cause Cs backward in time. The simplest way to rule out the possibility that effects cause their causes is just to stipulate that causes must precede their effects. Whether this is the best solution or even an acceptable solution is a good question for you to think about.

The signature feature of the regularity view is the third condition, which attempts to substitute for the proposition that causation provides a fundamental linkage among events. The success of the regularity view hinges on whether the third condition serves as an adequate substitute for causal oomph.

If you have a philosophical bent, the first question that should come to your mind is, "Adequate for what purpose?" In other words, what is a theory of causation supposed to do? Unfortunately, philosophers disagree about the answer to this question and are quite sensitive about the topic. Rather than boring you with my own unorthodox answer, I think it will be more productive for me to point out that contemporary philosophers tend to think we have a reasonably good pre-theoretical grip on some causal claims, and that a theory of causation should (1) agree with those claims while (2) helping us understand why they are true and while (3) making pronouncements about more controversial causal claims.

We routinely engage in this sort of intellectual activity. For example, we define 'addition' in arithmetic so that it corresponds to the answers that we know are correct and that we can often verify just by counting. If a computer calculates $432 + 51$ to be $10{,}758$, the right judgment to make is that the answer is wrong; we should not infer that the computer has discovered a previously overlooked marvel of arithmetic.

However, our attitude toward defining addition in more eso-
teric situations is rightly more forgiving. Can we add infinite
numbers, and if so, what rules govern such addition? Arguably, this is a matter to be settled by whatever serves the
purposes of mathematicians and scientists. It could turn out
that there are several useful but conflicting ways to define
addition for infinite numbers and that none of them is
uniquely best.

If we use this observation as a starting point, we can now
look at some cases where the regularity view of causation
does not seem to match up well with some relatively uncontroversial judgments about causation.

1. Often science relies on statistical evidence to attribute
    causation, and virtually all of this evidence points toward
    a probabilistic connection between event types, not a
    deterministic connection. Exposure to lead makes a child
    more likely to be convicted for a crime 20 years later
    (because it causes brain damage) but does not determine
    it. Because the regularity view requires absolutely every
    C to be followed by its E in order for causation to exist,
    it is at best unclear how it can accommodate our prac-
    tices regarding seemingly chancy causal relations.
2. The regularity view was defined by associating each indi-
    vidual c and e to respective types C and E. However,
    individual events can be assigned to a wide variety of
    event types. If we consider c and e very narrowly, as types
    C_n and E_n that incorporate the numerous microscopic
    details involved in how the very particular c and e are
    realized, it may well be that C_n and E_n occur only once
    in all of history. (Think how unlikely it is for the atoms
    in your body to be in the exact same arrangement at two
    separate times.) This has the consequence that the regu-
    larity view will wrongly judge almost every pair of con-
    tiguous events (narrowly construed) to be in a cause–effect
    relation. What's more, if we consider c and e very broadly,
    as types C_b and E_b that incorporate no details about them
    other than the size of the region they occupy and their
    location relative to one another, then again the regularity
    theory will judge that causation exists. After all, for any
    two times, t_1 and t_2, it is an exceptionless regularity that

if something happens at time t_1, then something happens at time t_2. The regularity view of causation is meant to apply mainly to medium-sized event types like "flipping a switch" or "beating a drum" that permit a reasonably wide range of different microscopic realizations but also apply only to small fragments of the universe. The problem is that it is not clear how the regularity view can restrict the allowed event types to chart an acceptable course between defining the events too narrowly and defining them too broadly, both of which result in an overabundance of causation.

3. The regularity view is too crude to distinguish when two events co-occur merely as effects of some common cause rather than standing in a cause–effect relation. When a low pressure front arrives, the reading on the barometer drops and then a rainstorm appears. Ignoring the issue of chanciness by imagining a perfectly reliable match between low barometer readings and rainstorms, the regularity view seems to imply that low barometer readings cause rainstorms. If you think low barometer readings can cause rainstorms, try to control the weather by forcing a barometer's needle to the lower setting.[1]

These three problems are partly responsible for the current unpopularity of the regularity view, but why would the regularity view be attractive in the first place? I believe much of the attraction can be traced to the worry that singular cause–effect relations cannot be objectively verified or experimentally observed. Such worries were on the mind of David Hume, so let's now examine what he had to say, keeping in mind that he may not have advocated what we are calling "the regularity view."

Hume's Causation

David Hume is arguably the most important historical figure for modern philosophical debates about causation. Hume grew up in Edinburgh, Scotland. His best-known works are

A Treatise of Human Nature, which he completed at age 26 in 1739, and a shorter work, *An Enquiry Concerning Human Understanding*, published in 1748, which discussed many of the same issues covered in the *Treatise*. Hume is associated with two famous philosophical doctrines, empiricism and skepticism, both of which impact his thoughts about causation.

First, empiricism is broadly speaking a philosophy based on the idea that knowledge of the world comes from experience. Hume claimed that all "objects of enquiry" could be partitioned into two groups: relations of ideas and matters of fact. Relations of ideas are propositions that are definitional or tautological. True relations of ideas include mathematical identities and conceptual truisms like "Green is a color." Matters of fact, by contrast, hold true at least partly based on how the actual world is constituted. For example, "Creatures do not live forever" and "Some maladies are contagious" are both true, but neither is true merely by definition. They are true partly because of the meanings of the terms used in the statement and partly because of biological reality.

According to a more technical philosophical definition, **empiricism** maintains that all knowledge about matters of fact is unattainable except through experience. Any truths that we could possibly come to learn without having any experience are relations of ideas and hence are merely definitional, not substantive truths that can be informative about the character of the actual world.

Second, skepticism is broadly speaking a philosophy emphasizing our lack of certainty about the world. In the modern philosopher's technical sense, **skepticism** is the claim that we know nothing about matters of fact. Skepticism can take more limited forms where it denies our ability to know some designated kind of fact. For example, a woman might be certain that her own thoughts exist and that time passes and that she maintains a continued existence through the passage of time, and yet she could be skeptical about the existence of an external world – denying that we know that there are material objects arranged spatially.

Another example of a limited form of skepticism is Hume's skepticism about causation. Hume suggested that no matter how much evidence we amass in favor of the claim that Cs cause *E*s, we can never know whether an observed instance of *C* forces an instance of *E* to occur, or whether instead *C*s are merely followed by *E*s without any deep metaphysical connection between them. He thinks causal oomph is undetectable in principle.

Hume combined empiricism and skepticism when he investigated the evidence we have for the existence of causation. An overly simplistic summary of his overall view is that because causal oomph is required for (our common sense construal of) causation but undetectable in principle, we are unjustified in believing that cause–effect relations exist objectively out there in nature independent of us humans. Hume is such an iconic figure in the history of causation, though, that we ought to dig into his writings in a bit more detail.

An initial observation to make about Hume's view is that it depends on his theory of psychology. Hume advocated what experts now call **associationism,** the doctrine that all our ideas are atomic thoughts or combinations of atomic thoughts. Ideas, according to Hume, do not have internal structure. For example, he notes that no one can really know what a pineapple tastes like without actually tasting one. Its taste, he thinks, is an unstructured psychological impression. We stick a chunk of pineapple in our mouths, and we get an impression of what it tastes like. After having lots experiences of different sounds, textures, colors, and so on, we are able to remember some of the impressions and arrange them in our mind according to a few simple psychological principles. For example, *remembering* a castle you have seen is just your mind activating a fainter version of your original visual impression of the castle. This raises the question of how people can ever entertain ideas about mythical creatures like centaurs, given that no one has ever seen a centaur. The answer is simply that because you have experienced men and horses, you are able to conjoin a mental image of the upper half of a man with a mental image of a horse's body.

Let's now see how Hume applies his associationism in part 7 of the *Enquiry* to the topic of causal oomph, what Hume calls a "necessary connection":

> When we look about us towards external objects, and consider the operation of causes, we are never able, in a single

instance, to discover any power or necessary connexion; any quality, which binds the effect to the cause, and renders the one an infallible consequence of the other. We only find, that the one does actually, in fact, follow the other. The impulse of one billiard-ball is attended with motion in the second. This is the whole that appears to the *outward* senses. The mind feels no sentiment or *inward* impression from this succession of objects: Consequently, there is not, in any single, particular instance of cause and effect, any thing which can suggest the idea of power or necessary connexion.

. . .

All events seem entirely loose and separate. One event follows another; but we never can observe any tie between them. They seem *conjoined*, but never *connected*. And as we can have no idea of any thing which never appeared to our outward sense or inward sentiment, the necessary conclusion *seems* to be that we have no idea of connexion or power at all, and that these words are absolutely without any meaning, when employed either in philosophical reasonings or common life. (Hume 1748, paras 50, 58)

Hume is saying that although we can see one billiard ball colliding with another and we can see them spreading apart afterward, the "tie between them" is imperceptible. So, even if there is some sort of causal oomph in action – something about the cause that makes the effect happen – we can never observe this causal oomph with our senses. Because none of us has ever experienced a "necessary connection," we literally cannot have the concept of a necessary connection. With regard to causal oomph, we are at best like sixteenth-century Eskimos, who had no conception of a pineapple's flavor.

After presenting this argument, Hume notes that there is a reasonable counter-response, which he advocates that we adopt. He says we can acquire the idea of a necessary connection by observing regularities between C and E and thereby acquire the habit of expecting the occurrence of an E after observing a C.

The first time a man saw the communication of motion by impulse, as by the shock of two billiard balls, he could not pronounce that the one event was *connected*: but only that it was *conjoined* with the other. After he has observed several instances of this nature, he then pronounces them to be *connected*. What alteration has happened to give rise to this new idea of *connexion?* Nothing but that he now *feels* these events to be connected in his imagination, and can readily foretell the existence of one from the appearance of the other. When we say, therefore, that one object is connected with another, we mean only that they have acquired a connexion in our thought, and give rise to this inference, by which they become proofs of each other's existence: A conclusion which is somewhat extraordinary, but which seems founded on sufficient evidence. (Hume 1748, para. 59)

For Hume, the only way we can acquire the idea of a necessary connection between Cs and Es is by interpreting the regularities in terms of our concept of a cause–effect relation.

We can summarize these conclusions by relating them back to the doctrines of empiricism and skepticism. The empiricism in Hume's theory is his commitment to the idea that we cannot learn whether Cs cause Es merely by mathematical or logical reasoning; we need to have experience of Cs causing Es. The skepticism in Hume's theory reveals itself in his conclusion that we cannot ever gain evidence that Cs cause Es because genuine causation requires a form of causal oomph – a necessary connection – and we cannot experience a necessary connection. At best, we can observe that Cs are always followed by Es.

There are several modern proposals that I will now mention as possible ways of interpreting Hume. Hume's precise view about causation is still controversial, and his writing is not maximally clear, so it is prudent to be cautious about attributing any of these following theories to Hume.

Projectivism

In everyday life, when people say you are projecting, that means you are unjustifiably or wrongly attributing a quality to someone else *because* you possess that quality. With regard to causation, projectivism is the theory that we humans mentally project the psychological compulsion that makes us expect an E when we observe a C onto the objects themselves.

Hume develops an analogy between causation and color. Our current science tells us that blue objects do not all share a common physical or chemical structure. There isn't any blueness in blue objects in the same (fundamental) way there is mass in all massive objects. Rather, the set of all blue objects is a heterogeneous collection of chemical and physical structures that are similar to each other because they produce the same kind of visual experience in most humans. People mentally project the psychological property of blueness onto external objects in the sense that we instinctively think of the blueness of blue objects as stuck in or on the objects themselves, not in our minds. Contrast blueness with how we think of mass as appropriately attributed to the objects themselves regardless of how we perceive their massiveness. Also consider how we think of pain. We project color onto the objects that cause us to experience color, but we don't project pain onto the objects that cause us to experience pain; the cactus does not contain any pain.

If we apply this to causation, Hume can be said to be a projectivist because at one point, (1748, ch. VII, sec. 60), he defines causation as "an object followed by another, and whose appearance always conveys the thought to that other." Hume here is referring to the psychological phenomenon that when we think of certain causes, we naturally think of their effects too. The compulsion to think of the effect when thinking of the cause is essentially an activity of the mind, and when we think of external events as bound by a necessary connection, we are attributing to the external events this feature of the mind, a "felt determination."

Causal Reductionism

Causal reductionism can be defined as the proposition that causation does not require any sort of causal oomph or any fundamental lawful connection among events. Hume seemingly endorsed causal reductionism when he defined a cause as "an object precedent and contiguous to another, and where all objects resembling the former are placed in like relations of precedency and contiguity to those objects, that resemble the latter." This definition is the inspiration for the regularity view of causation discussed earlier, and Hume has been interpreted as one of its early advocates.

Causal Realism

Philosophers have defined causal realism to be roughly the claim that causal relations exist out there in the world independently of how they are interpreted by humans or other human-like agents. Hume doubted that we will ever "penetrate so far into the essence and construction of bodies, as to perceive the principle, on which their mutual influence depends." In referring to this "ultimate connexion" or "operating principle" or "power by which one object produces another" Hume appears to believe that there is some sort of causation in the objects themselves, even though we can't possibly verify it.

Summary Evaluation

Let me now emphasize what I take to be the most important lesson. According to the regularity theory of causation, a cause does not *make* the effect happen. Events just happen. When the universe exhibits a pattern where every *C* is followed by an *E*, we are led to think of that pattern in terms of *C making E* happen, but in doing so we are drawing an inference that imputes more to the structure of the world than is actually there. We think of causes as exerting causal oomph, but we have no good reason to think causal oomph exists.

My advice concerning how to evaluate whether causal oomph exists is to recognize that this is a difficult task. It is just one special case of the general problem about how ontologically parsimonious one should be. In the philosophical jargon, 'ontology' refers to being or existing. To be ontologically parsimonious is to ascribe to the world very little fundamental structure. A famous philosophical declaration of support for ontological parsimony is Ockham's razor, the principle that one should not postulate entities beyond necessity.

The atomists I mentioned earlier are philosophers who had an ontologically parsimonious world-view. They believed the world is ultimately just atoms bouncing around in the void. The medium-sized objects of our everyday experience are not additional structure in the world, according to atomists; they are just atomic arrangements.

Although it is generally commendable to avoid unneeded components in a model of how the world is structured, one can take ontological parsimony too far. Sometimes, the posited structure is explanatory and avoids requiring fantastic coincidences in one's model of the world. Postulating vast conspiratorial arrangements of atoms, for example, can often be worse than postulating unnecessary entities. This is arguably the case concerning causation. The possible world H that consists of a mosaic of events in space and time is preferable on grounds of ontological parsimony to a possible world like F that consists of the same mosaic of events plus a fundamental dynamical law that governs how the events are arranged. But this fundamental dynamical law can reasonably be seen as *explaining* why the mosaic is arranged the way it is. In H, it is a remarkable but unexplained coincidence that the various states at various times satisfy a shockingly simple physics equation.

It is difficult to make any persuasive argument about how to weigh the virtue of ontological parsimony against the virtue of avoiding conspiratorial posits. As a result, standard arguments for and against causal oomph are not decisive. Here's a summary list to help you remember some considerations that go into making a decision about whether to believe in causal oomph. (These are my considerations, not Hume's.)

Advantages

1. The regularity theory does not appeal to allegedly mysterious linkages among events. Hume's main argument for (something resembling) the regularity view is that we can

observe and experimentally check whether C events are followed by E events, but we can never go a step further to
verify the existence of any causal oomph, or as he put it, "any
necessary connexion" between cause and effect. Thus, the
postulation of causal oomph goes beyond what any experience of the world can reveal to us. To adopt the regularity
view is to accept that we can do without this unobservable
structure in the world.

2.   The regularity theory permits a seemingly straightforward explanation of how we can attain knowledge of causal
regularities. Ideally, we can observe what happens where and
when, and since all facts about causation hold by virtue of
those observable facts, we can in principle safely draw inferences about causation.

Challenges

1.   The regularity theory treats the incredibly intricate
patterns in nature as fundamentally a matter of pure happenstance. Particles do not obey the laws of physics because
the laws of nature *make* them do it. Instead, there is just some
way particles happen to move around, and what we call
'laws' are really just convenient summaries of accidental patterns in the particle trajectories. This is arguably tantamount
to a conspiracy theory.

2.   The regularity theory makes causation depend on a
fundamentally arbitrary choice of how to group events into
types. This seems to make the existence of causation depend
on how the events are classified rather than on the character
of the events themselves.

3.   The regularity theory incorporates a troublesome
tension. On the one hand, if you look at nature in maximum
detail, the singular events are probably so intricate that it will
be unlikely that they will ever be repeated. On the other hand,
if you look at nature in an overly fuzzy way, you will end up
with explanations of why some event of kind E occurred, but
not of why the particular actual effect e happened.

4.   The regularity theory makes causation too extrinsic.
Whether c causes e depends on what patterns occur on the

far side of the universe. Because in practice these distant events are not observable, we cannot check whether they obey the right pattern. Thus, we are never in a good position to identify nearby cases of causation. To be justified, we would have to assume that events on the far side of the universe exhibit the same kinds of patterns as events around here, but that appears to conflict with the main motivation for the regularity view: that the pattern of events just occurs and is not *enforced* by any law of nature.

5.   The regularity theory does not have the resources to make sense of fundamentally chancy causation.

Questions

Q: It sounds like causal oomph is undetectable. So, it doesn't seem like there is any real answer to whether it exists. You're just going to keep going around in circles, aren't you?

A: You're right that causal oomph is undetectable, at least in the sense that if two worlds (like H and F) match with regard to their pattern of material facts and differ only in whether causal oomph exists, the inhabitants of those worlds will (by stipulation of the example) behave the same way and not be able to detect the causal oomph. But you have to be a bit careful here. There is a subtle issue of methodology at play that is worth exploring.

Let's take a scientific view of all of this by adopting the principle that the way to decide whether there is causal oomph is to base our decision on our best guess at an overall model of the universe. One principle that governs theory choice is ontological parsimony. The principle of ontological parsimony says that – all other things being equal – it is better to have a theory that postulates less structure. As Ockham said, "Do not postulate entities beyond necessity." F and H cannot be distinguished experimentally, and F differs from H by having some extra structure, the causal oomph. So it seems like we should prefer H over F.

But ontological parsimony is not the only principle for deciding among scientific models or theories. Another principle is that a theory or model is superior – all other things being equal – if it incorporates fewer coincidences. For example, imagine a theory claiming that five independent evolutionary processes in five ecologically different regions all resulted in tortoises with the same genetic makeup. Knowing some basic principles of evolutionary biology, we can conclude that it is highly unlikely that the very same species of tortoise would have arisen in so many different environments. The theory's invocation of a remarkable coincidence leads us to prefer models where tortoises evolved in one location and then migrated.

This raises a deep question about how to rank or weight the criteria used to evaluate scientific models and whether we have any decent grasp about what things are coincidental. I think a fruitful way to interpret the debate over causal oomph is to re-conceive of it as a debate about how we should decide among competing scientific hypotheses.

On the one hand, let's consider what some non-Humeans might argue. Remember, non-Humeans think there is something in fundamental reality beyond just a pattern of events in space-time, some sort of fundamental law that makes the universe develop through time with some extremely specific constraints on how matter can move around. They can say,

> Look around at the world our scientists have codified. To deny that there are laws at work and claim that there are just events here and events there is tantamount to claiming a massive coincidence. The Humean mosaic just so happens to be in complete accordance with the fantastically precise equations of physics without any exception. This is a textbook case of postulating a fantastic conspiracy.

On the other hand, Humeans can turn around and say the following:

> You claim that there are some fundamental laws of physics *making* the world develop a certain way, but that is just taking a metaphor too seriously. Laws of nature are not the kind of things that can push and pull material objects around or summon the future into existence. No matter how impressive

the hoped-for laws of physics turn out to be, they are fundamentally just equations that express how various parts of the actual world are related to one another. Equations are not the kind of thing that can engage in causation. What's more, calling them laws does not reduce the mystery. It just repackages the mystery under a new name. It doesn't explain the data any more than the hypothesis that the universe is the way it is because it was the will of God. Your appeal to laws is no more explanatory than postulating an undetectable ghostly spirit.

On the third hand, non-Humeans can come back and say the way science works is not to settle on what the Humean mosaic is and then debate whether the laws explain the Humean mosaic. In real science, the laws and the layout of matter are judged together as a package. We don't observe electrical charges and then ask whether we should explain these with a law or just a regularity. The only reason we believe particles can have electric charges is because we have laws that relate them to our scientific instruments in reliable ways. It is cheating to use the full package – Humean mosaic plus laws – to explain all the experiments and then to strip out the laws at the end as being unobservable. If you want to be an upstanding Humean, you have to explain experimental results without sneaking in any fundamental laws in your characterization of the data.

That was a long answer, but the important point here is that the debate about oomph is not merely about causation. It can also be seen as a debate about how to select among scientific hypotheses.

Q: There's this book I read called *Permutation City* where the main character at the beginning scans people's brains and inserts them into a virtual world where they are still conscious. And then he goes on to test whether they stay conscious even when he scrambles the order in which the computer actualizes each of the virtual guy's mental states. So the idea was that there is no causation from one computational state to the next, but so long as they all occur at some time or other, no matter how scrambled in time, the universe somehow automatically links together the various states and the person's conscious awareness automatically kicks in. Does that idea make any sense?

A: That's a brilliant example. I love it. So, two things come to mind. First, obviously there is no way to verify whether a creature on silicon is conscious. Second, setting that aside, what you have described captures the Humean point of view nicely and then takes it to a natural extreme. We saw how the regularity theory, besides having C and E events co-occur, also requires that they be spatio-temporally contiguous, with C happening before E. But why should *contiguity* matter from the Humean point of view? It is easy to see why people would tend to associate events using causal notions when they occur together in space and time because it is harder to observe distantly separated causes and effects. But, if causal relationships exist without having any fundamental causal oomph, as Humeans contend, what is the motivation for restricting the relevant patterns to ones where C and E are contiguous? We certainly do not have trouble *imagining* instances of causation without contiguity. Think of a wizard casting a spell that only takes effect after a three-hour delay. So is the contiguity requirement tacked on because the inter-actions that we happen to detect in the actual world appear to work in a continuous manner through time and space? Why should contiguity be considered essential to causation? That's a good question to think about.

Further Reading

There is no shortage of reading material on the topic of how reductive one's theory of reality should be. Psillos's (2009) essay is very accessible. On the topic of Hume's views on causation, I have found the introduction by Don Garrett's (2009) chapter on Hume to be excellent and short, and Helen Beebee's (2006) *Hume on Causation* to be excellent and more in depth.

Study Question

Lady Mary Shepherd wrote *An Essay upon the Relation of Cause and Effect* (1824), in which she attacks Hume's argument that we can coherently imagine an effect happening without any cause. In the two paragraphs that follow, she evaluates the thought experiment, imagining an object to just begin existing. For practice, express her argument in your own words and critically evaluate it. (Recall my third comment in the section on singular vs. general causation in chapter 1.)

> Let the object which we suppose to begin its existence of itself be imagined, abstracted from the nature of all objects we are acquainted with, saving in its capacity for existence; let us suppose it to be *no effect*; there shall be no prevening [= preceding] circumstances whatever that affect it, nor any existence in the universe: let it be so; let there be nought but a blank; and a mass of whatsoever can be supposed not to require a cause START FORTH into existence, and make the first breach on the wide nonentity around; – now, what is this starting forth, beginning, coming into existence, but an action, which is a quality of an object not yet in being, and so not possible to have its qualities determined, nevertheless exhibiting its qualities?

> If, indeed, it should be shown, that there is no proposition whatever taken as a ground on which to build an argument in this question, neither one conclusion nor the other can be supported; and there need be no attempt at reasoning. But, if my adversary allows that, no existence being supposed previously in the universe, existence, in order to be, must *begin to be*, and that the notion of *beginning an action* (the being that *begins* it not supposed yet in existence), involves a *contradiction in terms*; then this *beginning* to exist cannot appear but as a *capacity some nature hath* to alter the presupposed nonentity, and to act for itself, whilst itself is not in being. – The original assumption may deny, as much as it pleases, all cause of existence; but, whilst in its very idea, the commencement of existence is an effect predicated of some supposed *cause*, (*because the quality of an object* which must be *in existence to possess it*,) we must conclude that *there is no object which begins to exist, but must owe its existence to some cause*.

3
Process and Mechanism

In chapter 1, I mentioned two concepts that philosophers have invoked to capture the essential character of causation: *difference-making* and *production*. In this chapter, we are going to take an initial look at production by exploring some theories of causation based on causal processes and mechanisms.

There seem to be several main components to the idea of causal production. First, in order for causation to exist, one occurrence – the cause – must *bring about* another occurrence – the effect – where this bringing about is not merely a pattern in the history of the universe but where it exhibits causal oomph. Second, this causal oomph is asymmetric in the sense that a cause produces its effect without the effect also producing the cause. Ordinarily, this asymmetry is ensured by postulating that production operates only toward the future. Third, production is intrinsic in the sense that whether a given succession of events count as production does not depend on what is happening elsewhere in the universe. Fourth, production is thought to proceed in a spatially and temporally continuous manner. John Venn (1866, p. 320) suggested we should think of causation using the metaphor of *ropes* rather than *chains*.[1] The rope metaphor suggests that the continuity of production is exemplified in the local interactions among pulleys and levers. This continuity condition includes a requirement that the various stages in the causal rope satisfy the formal property of transitivity, the principle that whenever A produces B, which in turn produces C, A also counts as producing C.

Sadly, philosophers have not yet established any consistent terminology for classifying which accounts treat causation as genuinely productive. Instead, there appear to be several approaches that adopt a few features of production. (When philosophers appeal to productive conceptions of causation, it is often in the context not of laying out a comprehensive theory of causation but of exploring the causal relations between mind and body, which we will study in chapter 8.)

In this chapter, we will primarily examine two conceptions of causation that attend especially to the *continuity* aspect of productive causation. Causal process theories construe causation in terms of the continuous trajectories of objects through space-time and their collisions. Mechanistic approaches to causation focus on the explanatory practices of the special sciences as a way to identify an appropriate scientific conception of causation. Each can be studied mostly independently of the other. (There also exist two more conceptions of causation that have some productive aspects: manipulability and interventionist accounts. We will need to wait until chapter 7 before discussing these.)

As I see it, neither the causal process approach nor the mechanistic approach counts as a fully *productive* conception of causation because neither approach incorporates the "causal oomph" aspect of production. Causal process theories (and to a lesser extent mechanistic theories) are pattern-based, not influence-based. Recall Dummett's (1964) intelligent tree whose concept of causation is based merely on the observed pattern of events, ignoring any of the platitudes that incorporate agency. Causal process theories in particular adopt rules for evaluating the presence of causation that can be applied just using information gleaned from the history of the universe (including laws that are inferred from the observed patterns).

The approach based on determination that we will discuss later is arguably a better candidate for being considered genuinely productive, because determination accounts incorporate laws that provide a form of causal oomph and allow us to identify singular causes without knowing beforehand which specific effect occurred.

Causal Process Theories

Causal process theories build on the ancient hypothesis that fundamental reality is a complete history of material entities interacting with each other through crude physical contact forces. The recent prominence of these theories is due to a pair of exploratory transference theories of causation constructed by Jerrold Aronson in 1971 and David Fair in 1979. The idea that causation involves energy transfer was developed much more thoroughly by Max Kistler in 1999. Wesley Salmon in 1984 and Phil Dowe in 2000 revised these transference theories into what are now known as causal process theories.

Transference theories are based on the principle that causation involves the transfer of a physical quantity from one object to another. David Fair tentatively suggests the following schematic rule for when causation occurs:

> A causes B if and only if there are physical redescriptions of A and B as some manifestation of energy or momentum or [the A and B] refer to objects manifesting these that is transferred (flows), at least in part, from the A-objects to the B-objects. (1979, p. 236)

Consider a scenario where a billiards player strikes the white cue ball directly toward the solid green ball, knocking it into the corner pocket. Intuitively, the white ball's movement toward the green ball causes the green ball's movement into the corner pocket. Fair would account for this truth by noting that the white ball can be accurately described as having transferred energy and momentum to the green ball. Fair is optimistic that many instances of causation can be similarly reduced to a transfer of energy or momentum. In one of his examples, being angry causes a person to deliver a punch, and in principle, he suggests, there is a neurological story to be uncovered about how energy is transferred from the brain to the fist.

One recognized limitation of transference theories is the absence of causation when objects are not interacting. A rock flying through deep space (depicted as going left to right past a meter stick) is located at the left edge at one moment and at the right edge a second later. Intuitively, the rock's being at the left edge and having a relative velocity of one meter per second to the right is a cause of its being at the right edge one second later. Because there is no transfer of any quantity to another object, though, transference theories have the consequence that there is no causation in this free motion of an object through space. A name for the kind of causation that maintains the continued existence of things in their default inertial behavior is 'immanent causation'. What makes **causal process theories** different from transference theories is that causal process theories also include immanent causation as a genuine form of causation.

Causal process theories take their cue from Wesley Salmon's observation that there is a distinction to be drawn between a physical object moving through space and a spot of light moving across a wall. Einstein's theory of relativity is often (oversimplistically) interpreted as restricting the speed at which causation can take place. Causal processes, apparently, cannot travel faster than the speed of light in a vacuum, c. Salmon points out (in effect) that someone could erect a wall so far from a lighthouse that when the beam of light sweeps across the wall, the spot of light traverses the wall faster than c. Experts recognize that this faster-than-light motion of the bright spot on the wall does not violate relativity theory because a bright spot on the wall is not the kind of entity which is subject to the relativistic speed limit. Salmon wanted to state a criterion to distinguish entities that must obey the relativistic limits – causal processes – from entities that are not subject to the limit – pseudo-processes.

Crafting a theory that adequately distinguishes genuine causal processes from pseudo-processes appears to be the primary goal of causal process theories. The core strategy for explicating causation is first to use *processes* (rather than events or facts) and then to distinguish *causal* processes from *non-causal* processes when they possess the right kind of physical quantity. Accounts differ with regard to what counts as the appropriate quantity. In Salmon's theory, it is an object's ability to bear a mark; in Fair's theory, it is an object's energy or momentum; in Kistler's version, energy does the work; and in Dowe's theory, any conserved quantity will do.

It will be instructive for us to examine Dowe's theory, the Conserved Quantity (CQ) theory, in more detail because it is the most prominent reference point for causal process theories. It is based on two principles:

(CQ1). A *causal process* is a world line of an object that possesses a conserved quantity.
(CQ2). A *causal interaction* is an intersection of world lines that involves exchange of a conserved quantity.

A few other definitions help to make the theory more precise. Let's first attend to CQ1. An *object* is any item from science or common sense including spots of light and shadows. The *world line* of an object is its location through space and time. A *process* in general consists of all the object's properties along the world line of the object.

What distinguishes a causal process from a non-causal process is whether its corresponding object possesses a conserved quantity, a magnitude obeying a conservation law. Because a shadow moving across the ground does not possess a mass or a charge or momentum or anything like that, it is not a causal process according to the CQ theory. This is the correct answer because shadows are not subject to causal laws like the relativistic speed limit.

Does this appeal to conserved quantities correctly distinguish the kinds of processes that obey causal laws from those that do not? Wesley Salmon suggested a counterexample: A spot of light moving along the wall might be thought of as possessing energy, which is normally understood to be a conserved quantity.

Dowe argued in response that the reason that a moving spot of light does not count as a causal process is that it does not count as a process at all. A process, according to Dowe, is restricted to the properties in the history of an object that has a single identity through time. One putative kind of entity that does not count as an object is a so-called "time-wise gerrymander," like the pseudo-object consisting of the conglomeration of the coin in my pocket from time t_1 to t_2, the red pen on my desk from t_2 to t_3, and my wristwatch from t_3 to t_4. A moving spot of light on the wall, Dowe contends, is a time-wise gerrymander and thus its world line is not a process.

Distinguishing properly between causal and non-causal processes allows us to identify instances of immanent causation, the kind of causation involved when an object is merely persisting through time. A causal process is a chain (or rope!) of immanent causation.

In order to address non-immanent causation, we need to turn our attention to CQ2. When two objects like billiard balls collide, their paths through space-time are both bent at a location where they touch, as depicted in figure 3.1. As you know from your physics course, the momentum of an individual billiard ball changes when it collides, but the total momentum is conserved. That illustrates what Dowe means by an *exchange* of a conserved quantity. Momentum is a conserved quantity for the pair, but the momentum of each individual changes. Two processes exchanging such a conserved quantity constitutes a causal interaction.

Because momentum is conserved when macroscopic objects collide, most ordinary cases of causation are identified by the CQ theory as causal interactions. Furthermore, objects that are separated in space without any particles traveling from

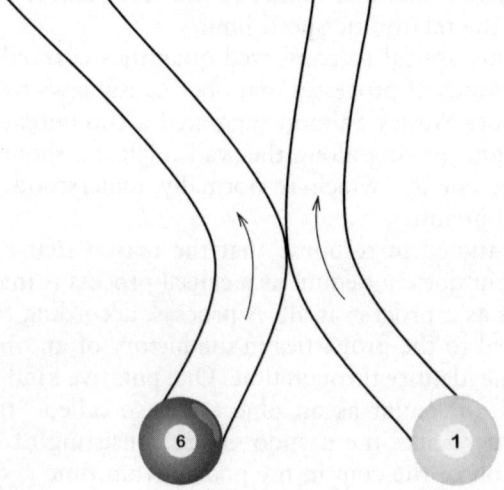

Figure 3.1

one to the other are identified as not interacting causally. To what extent the CQ theory's rules for assessing causal interactions can be deemed correct is difficult to say because it is not clear (to me at least) what tests the CQ theory's pair of principles is supposed to pass.

The final element in the CQ theory of causation is the conceptual link between causal interaction and causation. Causation is ordinarily understood to operate only toward the future, but there is nothing in the definitions to suggest what makes causation asymmetric. Dowe has advanced a theory about what makes causation asymmetric, but it does not derive the future-directedness of causation from the nature of conserved quantities; it instead relies on probabilistic relationships of the kind we will discuss when we study probability-raising accounts of causation. In any case, there is no standard explanation for causal asymmetry in causal process accounts.

Advantages

The arguments offered on behalf of transference and causal process theories include that they make causation objective and thus help to explain why our judgments about causation so often agree when we acquire all the relevant information.

Another cited advantage of causal process theories is that they only incorporate features of the actual world. Causation, insofar as it exists among public objects, should not depend on our choices about how to construe events, or how to rank the relative importance of multiple contributing causes, or what kinds of causal alternatives are worth attending to. Causal process theories are rare in not incorporating such subjective factors.

One demonstration[2] of the value of attending to causal processes in our judgments of singular (or token or actual) causation is the case of a probability-lowering cause. This is an example where the causal process theory produces an answer that most people judge to be correct, but where competing theories based on difference-making and probability struggle to produce the common sense judgment. Consider the toy theory of atomic decay depicted in figure 3.2.

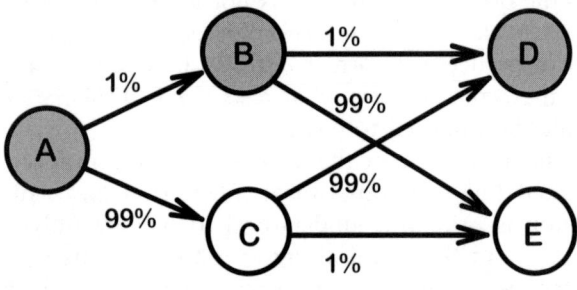

Figure 3.2

The circled A represents one type of radioactive element – call it A – that definitely decays within a few seconds and, when it does, has a 1 percent chance of becoming a different type of element, B, and a 99 percent chance of becoming a yet different type of element, C. Elements B and C are each capable of decaying into D and E elements according to the chances designated in the diagram.

Suppose we observe a case where an A decays into a B and then into a D with nothing else happening. It seems reasonable to recognize that B's existence helped to produce (and thus cause) D. After all, the only other way we could have gotten a D is by A decaying into C and then to D, but we know that did not happen because there never was a C in the scenario we are considering. But it is also true (from our initial perspective with A just sitting there) that the subsequent presence of B makes D less likely than it would have been if there had been no B. That's because if B had not existed, there would have been a C instead, and that would have made D 99 percent likely rather than the actual 1 percent chance D had at the intermediate time. This demonstrates that some causes lower the probability of their effects. (Later, we will investigate theories that associate causation with probability-raising, and this example will serve as a problem for them to overcome.)

Challenges

Causal process theories face a number of difficulties. Let's look at four of them.

1. In their current form, causal process theories are far too indiscriminate to be of much help in answering questions like "What causes autism?" They require all causes to be connected to their effects by continuously conveying the appropriate quantity, but this constraint is very weak in the sense that it doesn't classify many events as non-causes. An autistic person is composed of many molecules, each of which has recently collided with a vast number of other molecules in the nearby environment. Those in turn have recently collided with a vast number of other molecules in an even broader environment. Because molecules are almost always vibrating quickly and colliding with one another, just about everything in the past could be a partial cause of autism so far as the causal process theory is concerned. A pebble resting on the side of the road last month, the crowning of King Charles in 1266, the passing of a comet billions of years ago, are all linked via causal processes to current cases of autism. Yet it would be foolish to rearrange pebbles in an attempt to help prevent autism. Unfortunately, no causal process theory has yet provided a satisfactory account of which causal processes are relevant for purposes of prediction and control and explanation. Causal processes theories are not selective enough to distinguish which factors are relevant for curing disease, constructing gadgets, or increasing literacy. (Max Kistler's [1999] theory addresses this problem by appealing to laws of nature, but that in effect constitutes a significant departure from causal process theory.)

2. Causal process theories struggle to account for causal relevance and difference-making aspects of causation. Simultaneously adding blue dye and ice cubes to a glass of warm yellow lemonade will bring into existence a cool green liquid. Causal process theories correctly identify both additions as causes, but causal process theories by themselves do not identify the ice cubes alone as the cause of the coolness and the dye alone as the cause of the greenness.

A related example is causation by omission. Failing to be at the train station on time was a cause of your missing class, but the causal processes that make up your body did not exist at the train station. So how are they supposed to connect your non-existence at the station to your non-existence in the classroom in order to vindicate the claim that your lateness was a cause of your absence?

One promising solution to these problems is to supplement the causal process account with the kind of difference-making resources we will discuss in chapter 4. If this strategy succeeds, the resulting theory will have abandoned its originally intended role as a more objective account of causation than difference-making accounts, but perhaps a hybrid theory where difference-making is understood in terms of causal processes can achieve the original aims of the transference and causal process tradition.

3.   In order for causation to exist, according to the conserved quantity theory of causation, there must be conserved quantities. But it is not a far-fetched possibility that all the quantities that seem to be conserved are not perfectly conserved. Physicists often explore whether the quantities we call "fundamental constants" change somewhat over time. If we were to discover some fantastically small oscillation of energy, momentum, etc., causation would not exist according to the conserved quantity theory. But tractors would still pull, birds would still fly, and almost every activity that we think of as causal would still exist. This suggests a need for the conserved quantity account to explain why causation requires perfectly conserved quantities when all our evidence for causation apparently does not. No one has yet demonstrated how causal process theories can be properly insulated from the question of whether there are enough appropriate physical quantities.

4.   It is not clear how the theory applies when fundamental physics is not based entirely on particles that contact one another. In the Newtonian theory of gravity, for example, every mass attracts other masses without the need for collisions. If the world had such a gravitational force, the moon would not count as a cause of the tides according to the conserved quantity theory even though it ought to because it would still be tugging on the oceans according to a law that makes the tides come and go. Causal process theories, in effect, are predicated on the hope that nature does not include any fundamental fields, but only discrete particles. Either that, or causal process theories need to be extended beyond just particle world lines.

Further Reading

The canonical account of causal process theories is Dowe's *Physical Causation* (2000). A similar book-length discussion was written by Max Kistler (in French 1999, in English 2006). There are other process-based accounts that are not tied specifically to any physical theory, such as the one outlined in Ned Hall's (2004) article "Two Concepts of Causation," which argues that difference-making notions of causation conflict with the principle that causes need to be connected to their effects by the right kind of process. Similarly, purely process-based accounts struggle to accommodate the difference-making aspects of causation adequately. This suggests that there may not be a unified conceptual core for the cluster of causal principles we typically employ.

Study Questions

For practice, try to answer these two questions.

According to David Fair's theory, causation is not wholly objective but can depend on the frame of reference one chooses to adopt. In the rest frame of the billiard table, the white ball has positive kinetic energy that is transferred to the green ball, and thus it is the white ball that causes a change in the motion of the green ball. But in the rest frame of the white ball, it is the green ball that transfers its positive kinetic energy to the white ball, and so it is the green ball that causes a change of motion in the white ball. Thus, which ball is doing the causing depends on one's choice of perspective. Is this relativity of causal order a problem? (Dowe's theory tries to avoid this result by speaking of "exchange" rather than "transfer.")

In the atomic decay example depicted in figure 3.2, the presence of B lowered the probability of D from what it would have been if B had not existed (holding A's presence fixed). But one maneuver to resist the counterexample is to say that causation can proceed through causal links. The presence of A raised the probability of B above what it would have been without A, and B raised the probability of D above what it would have been without B (holding fixed the absence of C). Can you alter the example to address this adjusted theory of causation as probability-raising?

Mechanisms

Another recent line of philosophical research is based on the observation that *mechanisms* play an important explanatory role in the special sciences.

To the extent that special sciences like geology and neuroscience invoke causal relationships and causal laws, they are quite different from the laws of fundamental physics. Paradigmatic laws of fundamental physics relate microscopically specific states that extend far out into space. Paradigmatic causal relationships in the special sciences hold among fairly localized conditions that are not specified in maximum detail.

For example, a neuroscientist would not explain why the neuron emitted its neurotransmitter by citing the complete state of the universe and the fundamental physical laws. Even if the laws of physics govern the motion of all matter, such detail would not provide an informative explanation of what causes neurotransmitter emission. Nor is there an exceptionless law of neurotransmitter emission that a scientist could appeal to.

There is, however, a way of explaining neurotransmitter emission by describing it in terms of the interaction of its components. A neuroscientist might give an explanation along these lines:

> [A]n action potential depolarizes the axon terminal and so opens voltage-sensitive calcium Ca^{2+} channels in the neuronal membrane. Intracellular Ca^{2+} concentrations rise, causing more Ca^{2+} to bind to a Ca^{2+}/Calmodulin dependent kinase. The latter phosphorylates synapsin, which frees the transmitter-containing vesicle from the cytoskeleton. At this point, Rab3A and Rab3C target the freed vesicle to release sites in the membrane. Then . . . (Craver 2007, pp. 4–5)

and so on until the final stage, when the neurotransmitter is emitted.

I personally do not understand this explanation owing to my ignorance of organic chemistry, but it is clearly trying to account for how the emission of neurotransmitters works *by describing interactions among parts*. Non-scientists commonly explain by citing interactions among parts. To explain how a bicycle works, I recite a story about how the pedals, gears, chain, wheels, and frame work together to move the bicycle forward when the rider depresses the pedals. We can say those parts and their interactions constitute a mechanism that produces the bicycle's forward movement. Analogously, the axon depolarization, calcium binding, and so on constitute a mechanism that produces neurotransmitter emission.

How have philosophers fashioned a more precise conception of mechanisms? One convenient definition by Machamer, Darden, and Craver (2000, p. 3) equates mechanisms with "entities and activities organized such that they are productive of regular changes from start or set-up to finish or termination conditions." The connection between mechanisms and causation thus occurs through the concept 'production'. Mechanisms are normally understood to be reasonably well localized in space-time and operate only toward the future, as my earlier characterization of production indicated. To what extent mechanisms are thought to exert causal oomph is less clear.

One notable feature of this definition of mechanisms is its emphasis on general causation by referring to their being "productive of regular changes." Advocates for mechanistic accounts of causation do not emphasize the task of identifying singular causes – finding which particular causes explain a particular effect on a single occasion. The primary work of mechanisms is to explain *causal regularities*. For example, Stuart Glennan (1996, p. 52) defines a mechanism for a given type of behavior as "a complex system which produces that behavior by the interaction of a number of parts according to direct causal laws."

Mechanisms and Levels

According to Wesley Salmon's 1984 book, *Scientific Explanation and the Causal Structure of the World*,[3] a mechanistic explanation of some causal regularity identifies "black boxes" that connect an input state of affairs with an output state of affairs. The term "black box" designates a component of the explanation that is left unexplained. An explanation might declare that *I* produces *O* by way of *B*'s blocking the action of *D*. Such an explanation would say something about how components *B* and *D* relate but without explaining either of their internal structures.

Salmon endorses a causal process account of causation, and so, for him, explaining how the inputs produce outputs typically involves characterizing the causal processes connecting them. In most cases, inputs will be connected to outputs through many different causal interactions. Salmon calls a network of such interactions the "causal nexus." At the most general level of description, the causal nexus *constitutes* the mechanism that produces the output from the input. However, this nexus can usually be described at multiple levels of detail.

Let's apply this idea to a specific example. Suppose we want to explain why the population of London dropped by about 100,000 people in 1665. The input is the approximate population of London at the beginning of 1665, and the output is the approximate population of London at the end of 1665.

The simplest explanation for the reduced population is the Great Plague that struck London in early 1665. This explains the population loss by giving us information about what caused it, but it treats the plague figuratively as a black box by not revealing any details about how the plague operated.

A more thorough explanation would show us how the input connects to the output. On Salmon's account, we can open the black box we have labeled 'Great Plague' by describing the following events. Rats infected by the *Yersinia pestis* bacterium traveled to England on merchant ships. Fleas became infected when they bit infected rats. The infected fleas then bit humans and transmitted the infection to them. People also transmitted it to each other by coughing. The infection was severe enough to kill many humans. The cited causal mechanism includes causal processes (rats, ships, humans, fleas, bacteria) and the causal interactions where those processes intersect (bacteria infecting rats, rats traveling by ship, fleas biting rats, and so on). The input and output are connected by the interaction of all these processes, and identifying those interactions explains the population decline.

Someone could object at this point that we have not satisfactorily explained the population loss. It may be true, this objection goes, that people died when infected with *Yersinia pestis*, but that is just another black box. The input is a healthy person, the output is a plague victim, and the black box is the *Yersinia pestis* infection. We need a microbiological account of how *Yersinia pestis* interacts with the human immune system in order to explain how the plague produces victims.

It is easy to imagine that even with a more detailed account in hand, someone could demand a yet more detailed biochemical account of the mechanisms used by the bacterium to spread throughout the body. This leads naturally to the question, "Does mechanistic explanation bottom out?" That is, must there be some fully comprehensive explanation to which all others can delegate requests for more detail?

A conventional way to talk about this topic is in terms of levels. Explanations at the level of cellular biology can in principle be given mechanistic explanations at a lower level of chemistry, and chemical explanations can in principle be given mechanistic explanations at an even lower level of atomic physics. A mechanistic explanation accounts for phenomena at higher levels by relating it to mechanisms at lower levels. The ability of mechanistic explanations to provide further detail about how instances of causation are produced is one of their main appeals.

Bottoming Out

Unless there are infinitely many lower levels, we will eventually reach a point where the interacting parts have no parts themselves. Since we cannot explain these phenomena in terms of the interaction of their parts, we cannot explain them in terms of mechanisms. This level is often thought to be explained by fundamental physical laws instead

(Craver 2007; Machamer et al. 2000; Glennan 1996). When mechanistic accounts of causation reach this point, they are said to have bottomed out. Existing mechanistic accounts of causation all bottom out, but each proponent has handled the bottoming out differently.

Wesley Salmon advocates a causal process account of causation for the bottom level and uses that to explain mechanisms at higher levels. Salmon once advocated thinking of causation in terms of the capability of transferring marks but then later adopted a conserved quantity account of causation. He appears to treat mechanisms as a convenient way of talking about the macroscopic consequences of a fundamentally non-mechanistic account of causation, claiming that the mechanistic portion of his theory "furnishes something like a model of a telephone network that exhibits the lines of communication and the connections . . . It does not, however, reveal anything about the messages that are sent" (1997, p. 469). The messages here are the marks or conserved quantities of the causal processes, and these play the fundamental causal role in Salmon's account. Mechanisms play a derivative causal role in the sense that they are not productive but instead characterize the arrangement of the fundamental causal processes in a way that is explanatory.

Stuart Glennan has constructed an alternative approach to bottoming out that differs in two notable respects. First, he advocates an account of causation in which mechanisms in the special sciences play a substantive role in causation and do not merely summarize activities taking place on the bottom level. The laws governing the behavior of mechanisms are not in general *derived* from the laws of the fundamental level. Second, according to Glennan, there is some sort of causation at the level of fundamental physics, but he does not propose any hypotheses about how the world operates fundamentally.

To see the difference between these two ways of handling bottoming out, let's look back at (Salmon's) Great Plague example. Despite the significant differences in their accounts, a Glennan-style explanation of the Great Plague sounds largely the same as a Salmon-style explanation until it bottoms out in fundamental physics, at which point the different accounts of mechanisms and laws are paramount. Whereas

Salmon ultimately explains all causation mechanistically in terms of causal processes, Glennan abandons mechanistic explanation when explaining how fundamental physics is related to higher-level mechanisms.

The fundamental and mechanistic forms of causation that appear in Glennan's approach are similar in that they are both subject to laws. Glennan characterizes laws as generalizations that tell us how things would or could have happened had circumstances been other than they actually are. Fundamental physical laws qualify as laws under this definition, but so do more generic generalizations, like the regularities governing the behavior of water valves or the spread of disease.

Should mechanistic accounts of causation *depend* on the account of causation that applies at the most fundamental level? According to Glennan, we are entitled to answer "No" because we evaluate the truth of our causal claims by referring to mechanisms, not to fundamental physical laws. For example, the truth of "*Yersinia pestis* caused the population of London to fall by 100,000" does not depend, says Glennan, on any particular arrangement of fundamental physical interactions. It depends only on whether *some* appropriate mechanism links *Yersinia pestis* to the population decline. Mechanisms may be compatible with fundamental physical interactions and less precise, but we look for mechanisms when we look for causal explanations.

Glennan takes the irreducibility of mechanisms as evidence that the level of fundamental physical phenomena is crucially different insofar as causation is concerned. No doubt, the kind of behavior exhibited by very tiny particles differs from our observations of causation in our everyday lives. According to Glennan, quantum phenomena seem strange to us precisely because we have not identified any causal mechanisms to explain them. If no such mechanism exists, quantum phenomena will remain strange to us, even if we can provide an adequate non-mechanistic account of causation to explain them. But even if the curious behavior of the quantum world requires a non-mechanistic account of causation, that is no reason, says Glennan, to reject the mechanistic account of causation insofar as it applies to the behavior of larger objects.

Advantages and Challenges

Unlike most other approaches to causation, the mechanistic approach is less the subject of specific complaints and more the subject of questions about what a mechanistic theory of causation is supposed to do. Advocates for more emphasis on mechanisms have not yet clarified which problems the concept of a mechanism is not intended to address. The appeal to mechanisms certainly plays a noteworthy role in our *understanding* of causation. Scientists often *interpret* and *explain* the world's behavior in terms of causal mechanisms, and so any philosophical exposition of how various sorts of explanation relate to one another and to causation needs to clarify a concept (or multiple concepts) of mechanism.

Yet there are other philosophical tasks, like explaining how various causal regularities are related to fundamental reality, that advocates for mechanistic approaches do not address. Few constraints on the nature of a mechanism have been defended. For example, must mechanisms involve only local interactions or can they include some sort of action at a distance? Must every causal regularity involve a mechanism? What is the relationship between singular causation and mechanism? Without any definitive constraints, the concept of a mechanism might be too general to guide research on causation. The challenge here is to make more precise what questions the appeal to mechanisms can possibly help to answer.

Questions

Q: If it is so unclear what mechanistic theories are supposed to be doing, why are we even talking about them?

A: I mentioned them because mechanisms are one of the most important ways to explain a *causal regularity*. If you can humor me for a moment, I will give you my own take on why it is useful for us to use the concept of a mechanism when thinking about general causation.

In brief, mechanisms are the hidden structure inside causal regularities. In order to explain what 'hidden structure' amounts to in this context, let's first distinguish between natural and artificial kinds.

A **natural kind** is a category whose extent is not entirely determined by the linguistic or conceptual choices we humans make. A paradigmatic example of a natural kind is gold. Long before the periodic table of the elements was constructed, people knew that there was a substance with distinctive properties; in its pure form, it is yellowish, very shiny, attractive, and soft. People also knew that some gold did not have these properties and some non-gold did have these properties. On the one hand, gold can be tarnished or lying unmolested as ore. On the other hand, pyrite is shiny, yellow, and attractive, yet only fools identify it as gold. What this shows is that people's concept of gold, even going way back in time, is of a substance with a *hidden nature* whose presence can be checked using careful measurements (for example, of its density or its reaction to acid). The hidden nature of a natural kind is something that we can investigate scientifically. In the case of gold, we eventually discovered that gold is an element with 79 protons. Nothing else is genuine gold.

For contrast, consider the artificial category of games. Like gold, games have certain paradigmatic features: they are enjoyable, they have winners and losers, and they have rules. Like gold, many instances of games do not exhibit these features. A game of fetch with a single dog is not competitive, a game of make-believe is largely unconstrained by rules, and baseball is paradigmatically boring. What makes a game an artificial kind is that we know from the outset that no scientific investigation is going to identify the hidden nature of games. Games constitute a category that cannot have a hidden nature. The set of games can be expanded and contracted as we humans choose, but it is pointless for a scientist to investigate whether dancing is a game that people have mistaken for a non-game or whether tag is a non-game that people have mistaken for a game. Although science might uncover previously unrecognized principles governing which activities people find enjoyable, the concept of a game makes it impossible *by definition* to find an underlying feature of games themselves that distinguishes them from non-games. All there is to being a game is being a member of the set of things people choose to designate as games.

How does this apply to mechanisms? A causal mechanism can be thought of as the hidden nature underlying a given causal regularity. How was it that rats caused Londoners to die? Not because of a law relating rats and Londoners. Instead, there was a scientifically discoverable (but originally hidden) detail: the mechanism that involved fleas, *Yersinia pestis*, and everything else mentioned in the explanation of the Great Plague.

Similarly, how is it that restricting people's diet to wood and grass causes them to become malnourished? Because of the scientifically discoverable chemical structure of wood – that it is mainly cellulose – and the scientifically discoverable biological nature of humans – ensuring that cellulose will not be digested by humans. To spell out the details is to specify the causal mechanisms present in human digestion.

I am making the positive suggestion here that mechanisms are explanatory in part because (by definition) they characterize causal regularities (1) in more detail than is provided by merely citing causes and effects, and (2) in a way that typically has the effect of implying the existence of other causal regularities. These additional regularities include those that allow us to diagnose the presence or absence of the hypothesized mechanism and regularities that allow us to intervene and disrupt the causal regularity. For example, the cited explanation of the Great Plague suggests very strongly that if you were to test fleas for susceptibility to infection by *Yersinia pestis*, you would find that they are capable of being infected, and that if there had been some way to eradicate the fleas, the contagion could have been prevented.

In my mind, these two features of mechanisms are enough to vindicate their explanatory value and to make their widespread existence in virtually every scientific field unsurprising. The benefit of thinking about mechanisms as the hidden nature of a causal regularity is that it does not require that mechanisms (1) be part of fundamental reality or (2) engage in causal production, or (3) be absolutely required for causation.

Further Reading

Anyone researching mechanisms and their relation to causal explanation should review Machamer et al.'s (2000) "Thinking about Mechanisms," and Craver's (2007) accessible *Explaining the Brain* and (2005) "Beyond Reduction: Mechanisms and Multifield Integration and the Unity of Neuroscience." Glennan's (2009) chapter on causal mechanisms in the *Oxford Handbook of Causation* provides an excellent summary of the issues at a more advanced level, and it is important to look at his (1996) article "Mechanisms and the Nature of Causation," as well as Hitchcock's (1995) and Salmon's (1997) exchange in "Salmon on Explanatory Relevance" and "Causality and Explanation: A Reply to Two Critiques."

4
Difference-Making

I have a story for you. Actually, a fragment of a story . . .

> When Kundra placed the Yndari cube on the platter for the K-bot to probe its interior structure, she mentally scribbled a hypothesis: Given its ability to project infrared images through the slender crack in its carapace – largely of Ynari troop movements and surveillance footage – there is probably a micro-antenna and some crystalonics for image processing. The report from the K-bot, however, trounced her prognostication with its simplicity and perplexity. The Yndari artifact was entirely empty! Inside its twisted metal shell was just air: a mundane mixture of oxygen and nitrogen. The cube was altogether without any mechanism, though squeezing it reliably toggled video projections of remarkable clarity and independently confirmed accuracy. (Excerpt from *The TrainStar Legacy*)

If we only take into account the external characteristics of the Yndari artifact, it is reasonable to conclude that its activation *causes* images to appear, yet when the interior is examined, there is no apparent *causal mechanism*, no relevant connection between the squeezing of the Yndari cube and its emission of light.

In chapter 3, we surveyed some philosophical speculations about how to understand causation in terms of production, process, and mechanism. The question now up for consideration is this: Is there an adequate way to characterize causation without production?

There is at least one good reason for thinking that causation requires some underlying mechanism. Virtually anytime we investigate reliable causal connections between Cs and Es, we find some physical stuff – forces, masses, fields – that instantiate a continuous connection from C to E. (Quantum mechanics is sometimes alleged to exhibit a "spooky" form of influence that has no mechanism, but that's too tricky for us to debate here.)

There is also an argument to be made that causation does not *require* mechanisms. We frequently learn about causal relationships without knowing anything about underlying mechanisms. We frequently treat processes as black boxes whose internal details are largely irrelevant to their behavior. For example, when we press the 'R' key on a computer keyboard, it *causes* an 'R' glyph to appear on the screen. Yet we know that there is no unique route required for the electrical signals to bring about the effect. So long as we know there is a reliable-enough linkage between the pressing and the appearance, we are in a good position to infer a cause–effect relation.

In this light, Kundra's puzzlement over the Yndari cube should make perfectly good sense to us. The artifact can be reliably operated to project images at will simply by squeezing it on and off. So, macroscopically, it is as causal as can be. Yet, when its interior is examined, there does not appear to be anything that could explain how it works, so it defies the seemingly regular pattern in nature that all causation proceeds through some sort of mechanism.

Our task now is to see whether we can make sense of causation in a way that does not depend on causal mechanisms or production.

Most prominent accounts of causation provide some sense in which causes make a difference to their effects. The importance of difference-making to causation is largely motivated by our observation that causation does not strictly speaking require the existence of any underlying mechanisms. If squeezing the artifact reliably makes a difference to whether it projects images, that is causation enough. Or at least, that is the guiding idea behind difference-making theories of causation. The lack of any circuitry or antennae is surely surprising, but if we are nevertheless convinced that a squeeze makes a difference to the artifact's emission of a video, we should be convinced that the squeezes *are causing* the artifact to operate.

The general idea of difference-making has been articulated in several forms. In this chapter, we will explore the idea of measuring difference-making in terms of what is called 'counterfactual dependence'. Then, in the next two chapters, we will look at other ways to make sense of 'making a difference'.

Counterfactual Dependence

Much of the past hundred years of philosophy has invoked linguistic structures to help investigate concepts like causation. For a classic example from the philosopher Nelson Goodman (1947), we can imagine a scenario in which a person strikes a match, causing it to light. If we try to express how the striking of the match made a difference to the match's lighting, we might say (correctly), "If the match had not been struck, it would not have lit." Statements of this form are called 'counterfactual conditionals' because they make a claim about how things would or could have turned out differently if, contrary to fact, the specified condition had obtained. Counterfactuals are often expressed in the form, "If *A* had happened, *B* would have happened." Any difference-making account of causation that identifies or quantifies difference-making in terms of prescribed counterfactual conditionals is called a counterfactual account of causation.

The canonical version of the counterfactual account is presented in David Lewis's (1973a) article "Causation," which I will now summarize with some minor modifications that help me understand what is going on.

The game, as most philosophers understand it, is to construct a theory that (1) will take as input a scenario that includes a target event *e* that serves as the effect and (2) will produce as output some events in that scenario that count as "the causes of *e*." The quality of the theory is measured primarily by how well this function reproduces common sense judgments of e's causes in that scenario. Secondarily, a theory should avoid being unreasonably complicated and should generate its output using concepts like chance, time, and natural law rather than merely fitting the data with ad hoc parameters.

For a classic example (McLaughlin 1925, p. 155), consider two independent agents attempting to assassinate a desert traveler. The first poisons the contents of the traveler's canteen while the second creates a small leak in the canteen. During the journey, the poisoned water leaks out and the traveler dies of thirst. We can choose our target event e to be the death of the traveler. Intuitively, one of the causes of e was the leak created in the canteen. The introduction of poison is intuitively not one of the causes of e. To get this example right, a theory of causation is supposed to identify the leak as a cause of e and the poisoning as a non-cause of e.

Recall that it is important for the scenario not to be characterized with loaded terminology that would beg the question of what the causes are. For example, if the second agent's activity had been described in the scenario as an assassination, one could quickly infer that he caused the death merely by recognizing that, *by definition*, assassination implies that the assassin was a cause of the victim's demise.

In Lewis's proposed account, we are supposed to assume that a substantial number of counterfactual conditionals have truth values we can readily ascertain by considering how reasonable they sound. These include counterfactuals that draw relationships among the occurrence of events in scenarios that are not too far-fetched. We identify the causes of some chosen e in some chosen scenario using the following procedure:

1. We consider all the events in the scenario that could possibly serve as candidate causes of e.
2. For each candidate cause, c_i, there is a proposition, $O(c_i)$, which is the claim that the event c_i occurred in the given scenario. Similarly, $O(e)$ is the proposition that event e occurred in the scenario.
3. We now evaluate the truth value of two counterfactual conditionals: "If $O(c_i)$ had been true, then $O(e)$ would

have been true," and "If $O(c_i)$ had been false, then $O(e)$ would have been false."

4. In cases where both of these counterfactual conditionals are true, we say that the proposition $O(e)$ **counterfactually depends** on the proposition $O(C_i)$. Otherwise, we say that $O(e)$ does not counterfactually depend on $O(c_i)$.

5. If $O(e)$ counterfactually depends on $O(c_i)$, we say that the event e **causally depends** on the event c_i. Otherwise, we say that e does not causally depend on c_i.

6. If some chain of causal dependence relations exists from c_i to e, we declare c_i to be one of the causes of e and that causation holds between c_i and e. If no chain of causal dependence exists, we say that c_i is not a cause of e.

In trying to understand this procedure, it helps to make two observations about the conceptual setup. First, I have deliberately followed Lewis in distinguishing between an *event* and the *proposition* (or statement) that that event occurred. This is noteworthy because in Lewis's theory, the logic governing counterfactual conditionals in ordinary language provides a structure that is intended to restrict which counterfactual dependencies hold. (In the same year as his article on causation, Lewis published a book characterizing a family of counterfactual logics, and defending several logical rules that apply to ordinary language counterfactuals.)

For example, any counterfactual conditional of the form, "If P were true, then Q would be true" has the same truth value as Q in cases where P is true. After a round of cards, one player might misperceive his partner's cards and say, "If you had drawn an ace, you would have won." The partner, knowing that she drew an ace and lost, can respond truly, "That's incorrect. I drew an ace and lost anyway." The mere fact that P was true and Q was false gave her enough information to infer the falsity of "If I had drawn an ace, I would have won." Later, we will look at one problem generated by using the logic of ordinary language counterfactuals to evaluate causal dependence rather than constructing a non-linguistic measure of difference-making. But for now, just note that the first counterfactual in step 3 is automatically true because the occurrence of both events is guaranteed by the mere fact that we are considering events that we are presupposing have occurred. So the existence of counterfactual dependence hinges only on the second counterfactual.

Let's refocus on the basics now by returning to our desert traveler example and seeing how well Lewis's account fares at producing the desired output. The goal for the theory is to pronounce that the introduction of poison into the canteen was not a cause of the traveler's death, but the introduction of a leak in the canteen was.

Let's first consider the poisoning event, c_1. It seems that if the assassin had not poisoned the water in the canteen, the canteen would still have the same leak it actually had. After all, the two assassins were acting independently. Thus, the traveler would still have died of thirst. The only difference would have been that drinkable water would have leaked rather than poisoned water. The falsity of "If the assassin had not poisoned the canteen, the traveler would not have died" implies that there is no causal dependency of e on c_1, no direct causation from c_1 to e. But we also have to ask whether there are any chains of causal dependence. To answer this question, we attempt to think of any intermediate events that might causally depend on c_1 and that e might causally depend on. For example, we could consider p_1, the presence of poison in the canteen. Event p_1 does depend causally on c_1 because if the assassin had not introduced poison into the canteen, its water would still be drinkable. But e does not appear to depend causally on p_1. If the water had not contained poison, the traveler would still have died because the contents would have leaked just the same. So it is false that, "If p_1 had not occurred, e would not have occurred." So there is no chain of causal dependence that we have found yet. If we cannot think of any other intermediate events that form a chain of causal dependence, we should conclude that c_1 is not a cause of e, which is the result we were looking for. I personally can't think of any right now, so I am going to accept tentatively that Lewis's scheme correctly identifies c_1 as a non-cause.

Our second task is to consider the event, c_2, where the canteen is made to slowly leak its contents. It seems reasonable to judge that if the second assassin had not poked a hole in the canteen, the canteen would have contained poison later when the traveler was first growing thirsty. Assuming the traveler would have drunk from his canteen as he traveled across the desert, he eventually would have died of poison rather than thirst. That makes it false to say, "If the second assassin had not introduced a leak into the canteen, the traveler would not have died." The falsity of that counterfactual implies that there is no causal dependency of e on c_2, no direct causation from c_2 to e. But unlike the previous case, there is arguably an intermediate event that causally depends on c_2 and that e causally depends on. Let us say that d is an event where the canteen is empty and dry some time shortly before e. It seems reasonable to think the following is true: "If the assassin had not produced a leak in his canteen, then the canteen would not have been dry." (It presumably would have been filled with the poison instead.) So d causally depends on c_2. It also seems reasonable to think the following counterfactual is true: "If the canteen had not been dry, e would not have occurred." That is, his actual death (of thirst) would not have occurred without the empty canteen. So e causally depends on d. Because there is a chain of causal dependencies going from c_2 to e, c_2 is a cause of e. This conclusion vindicates the common sense observation that the traveler's death was caused by the leak introduced into the canteen and not by poison. So the theory appears to generate the right answers for this scenario.

The causal dependencies in this example can be illustrated using what is called a neuron diagram (figure 4.1).

In a neuron diagram, the circles designate a possible event, a shaded circle designates an actual event, an arrow from one actual event to another actual event indicates a relation of causal dependence, and a continuous sequence of arrows

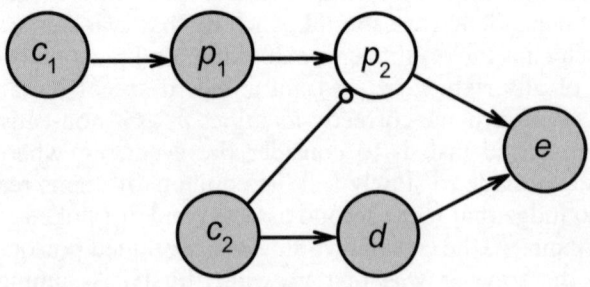

Figure 4.1

going from shaded circle to shaded circle means that each of the events is a cause of all the events further along the graph. For example, c_1 is a cause of there being poisoned water in the canteen shortly afterward, p_1, but p_1 is not a cause of there being poisoned water in the canteen a couple of days later, p_2, because p_2 did not occur. The introduction of the leak, c_2, successfully blocked p_2 from occurring, indicated by the line segment with the circular arrowhead. The main task we set for ourselves was to identify the causes of e, and you can easily trace backward from e through the arrows to find that d and c_2 were causes and the others were not.

I deliberately did not approach this example with a critical eye because later we will ferret out some deficiencies in the reasoning I just used. But for now, I will just point to one potential source of mischief. The argument that c_1 was not a cause of e spoke of e as if it were equivalent to "the death of the traveler," while the argument that c_2 was a cause of e spoke of e as if it were equivalent to "the death of the traveler by thirst." This difference played a crucial part in the reasoning. When we counterfactually eliminated the poisoning from our scenario, we kept the leak and inferred a death by thirst. When we counterfactually eliminated the intermediate d, we inferred no death by thirst. But maybe we should have inferred that if the canteen had not been dry, it would have been filled with poison, so that the traveler would still have died, but not from thirst. If e includes the possible death by poisoning, the argument does not succeed. So there was an implicit assumption that the correct way to evaluate the relevant counterfactuals was to use a more narrowly circumscribed e.

In the technical jargon, one speaks of the fragility of an event,[1] which characterizes how much an event is allowed to change qualitatively before it no longer counts as the very same event. Arguably, every event that occurs in the physical world is realized with a precise arrangement of microscopic particles. We ordinarily do not care about the very particular way events are realized. We think that if one molecule in the victim's body were counterfactually shifted slightly, the death would still have occurred but in an ever so slightly different way. But when the hypothetical alterations to an event become too great, we react differently. If the traveler had survived the trip across the desert and succumbed to influenza seventy years later, then we would not declare c_2 to be a cause of his death. We would say the e in the previous example did not even occur. When just about any slight hypothetical alteration to an event makes it count as "not the same" event, we say the event is extremely fragile. When an event can be altered somewhat but not too much and still count as "the same" event, we say it is moderately fragile. When an event can be altered significantly in many diverse respects, we say it is not fragile. The relevance of fragility to causation, at least insofar as standard counterfactual accounts are concerned, is that effects need to be characterized at a moderate level of fragility: too fragile and virtually every previous event will count as a cause; not fragile enough and there will be scenarios where too few causes are identified correctly as genuine causes. I will describe an example later, but you may want to pause and think of one yourself as an exercise.

To summarize, we have now seen one way to evaluate counterfactual dependence and thereby causation. A notable feature of this method was that it relied on a counterfactual logic with a binary characterization of counterfactual conditionals as either true or false. There are no degrees of counterfactual dependence in Lewis's model and thus no degrees of causal dependence. It also construed causation as transitive by defining causation to include any chains of causal dependence. This feature was needed to derive the result that the traveler's death was caused by the leak. It was also important that the traveler's death was characterized with moderate fragility: not specified too broadly as any kind of death and not specified too narrowly as the microscopically specific death that actually occurred. When we later examine obstacles for counterfactual accounts, these three components will be subject to criticism. For the moment, though, let us stay positive by surveying why a counterfactual account of causation might be attractive.

Advantages

1. I began this chapter by pointing out one apparent benefit of a counterfactual account of causation. It makes sense of

how we can identify causal relationships even when we are not in a position to evaluate whether there is an underlying mechanism connecting the cause to the effect.

2. A related advantage is that empiricists, who are doubtful that we can ever have good evidence for causal oomph, can take solace in the fact that counterfactual theories do not require any causal oomph. So long as there is enough structure in fundamental reality to vindicate the truth or reasonableness of the counterfactual conditionals bearing on causal claims, causation will exist. For this reason, counterfactual conceptions of causation are considered friendly to a Humean conception of causation.

3. However, I think there is a better reason to believe that counterfactual theories are getting at something deep about the nature of causation, namely that *causes affect*. It is helpful here to draw a distinction between changing the future and affecting the future. For some event c to affect the future is (by definition) for c to help make the future different from the way the future would have been if c had not happened. For some event c to change the future is (by definition) for c to make the future different from the way the future will actually be. A few moments of meditation on the definition of "change the future" should wrinkle some brows. If the future just is the way things turn out, how can I make that future different from itself? If I make the actual future not happen, then it wasn't the actual future to begin with. If I make some alternative future become the actual future, then it was not an alternative future to begin with. These sorts of considerations are meant to suggest that the idea of changing the future (as I have just defined it) is incoherent. The idea of affecting the future, by contrast, makes sense because it involves a contrast between a single actual future and some hypothetical alternative future. My reason for thinking that causation requires some sort of counterfactual dependence is that *affecting is inherently counterfactual*. To affect is to make things different from the way they would have been. So, if causes affect at all – which they do – they affect counterfactually. That doesn't mean that we have to use the grammar or logic of ordinary language counterfactual conditionals, but it does mean that causation somehow implicates a form of difference-making that contrasts the way things

actually happened to the way things would have happened or could have happened.

4.   We can make the observation that "causes affect" more concrete by considering causation by omission, which is what happens when a non-occurrence or absence or prevention or failure counts as a cause. For example, when Jack fails to set his alarm clock and consequently sleeps through his first class, it is natural to observe that Jack's failure to set his alarm clock was one cause of his missing class.

Causation by omission is widely viewed as a problem case for accounts of causation that require the existence of production or mechanism. The worry is that a non-occurrence is not the kind of event that can produce anything. After all, it doesn't exist. Counterfactual accounts of causation, by contrast, seem to resolve causation by omission quite easily. To see how, all we need to do is note that the following counterfactual is true: "If Jack had not failed to set his alarm clock, he would not have missed class." Because missing class causally depended on the failure, the failure was a cause of missing class. Done!

Well, let's not be so hasty. Although counterfactual theories make sense of how omissions can count as causes, they do so in a way that makes it easy for events to count as causes. Lots of non-occurrences – call them 'negative events' – will count as causes. For example, choose some unremarkable effect like the blooming of some flower. What caused the flower to bloom? One of the causes was the absence of any meteor crushing it earlier. If a meteor had not failed to strike the flower, the flower would not have bloomed. Another cause was the lack of a deer eating the flower bud. Another cause was the lack of a unicorn eating it. As you can easily imagine, a multitude of negative events count as causes of the flower's blooming if we judge causation using counterfactuals in the manner just prescribed.

Sarah McGrath (2005) has made an argument more generally that either (we should understand causation so that) omissions are never causes, or (we should admit that) omissions are far more prevalent as causes than common sense makes them out to be.

One possible response (Davidson 1967; Beebee 2004) is to argue that although omissions cannot cause anything, we mention them as causes because they are part of a more comprehensive causal explanation. Citing an omission helps to place other actual causes in context. McGrath points out that this response does not provide enough resources to draw the needed distinction between omissions that are causally culpable for the effect and omissions that are not.

Another possible response from an advocate of counter-factual theories of causation is to suggest that a distinction should be drawn between bona fide events and non-events so that the vast majority of omissions count as non-causes on the ground that they do not even count as events. However, this strategy is extremely difficult to carry out successfully without continually invoking unprincipled (ad hoc) choices about where to draw the boundary between negative events and non-events.

Yet another possible response (from an advocate of counterfactual theories) is to accept that the negative events are all genuine causes but then explain why we do not normally cite them in causal explanations. It is true that the lack of a hungry unicorn nearby was one of the causes of the flower blooming, but it is almost always uninformative to cite the absence of unicorns because it applies to all blooming events and thus does not tell us anything particular to this one flower.

Unfortunately, this last strategy is also deficient because it proves too much. If the philosopher's game allows us to count a multitude of events as bona fide causes and then explain why we do not normally think of them as causes by appealing to pragmatic considerations (like the uninformativeness of citing them), then we could ask why the counterfactual theory deserves credit for counting the poisoning of the canteen as a non-cause. For it is all too easy to declare that poisoning the canteen was a genuine cause of the traveler's demise, *e*, and to explain why, for various practical reasons, people tend to think of it as a non-cause. For example, the fact that the traveler showed none of the usual effects of poison is a good reason for thinking that *e* did not exhibit the particular kind of death that usually occurs when poison is the *main* cause of death. Nevertheless, these facts do not constitute evidence for the poisoning being a non-cause of *e*; they are evidence for the poisoning being an unremarkable, unexplanatory, and ignorable cause of *e*.

The lack of a clear distinction between genuine non-causes and events that are genuine but insufficiently noteworthy causes points toward a troubling lack of rigor in philosophers' standards for what counts as an adequate theory of causation. If an advocate of a counterfactual theory of causation is permitted to explain away common sense judgments about non-causation, then why not go further and just adopt the simplest theory of causation ever? Here is a definition for the simplest theory of causation: For any event *e*, and any event *c*, *c* is a cause of *e*. In a slogan, the simple theory of causation proclaims, "Everything is a cause of everything." When presented with the counterexample of a *c* and *e* that have nothing to do with one another, the advocate of the simple theory of causation can trot out his pat response: "Sure, there are lots of good reasons why people tend to think of *c* as not being a cause of *e*, but those reasons are merely pragmatic. They explain why *c* is not worth citing in causal explanations of *e*, why *c* is not a good means for bringing about *e*, why knowledge of *c* does not help anyone predict *e*'s occurrence, and so on. But for all that, *c* is still a cause of *e*." I suspect that there is a lot to be gained from thinking about how one should respond to the simplest theory of causation.

Challenges

Now, having flagged the main advantages of counterfactual theories of causation, let's take a look at some of the main criticisms that have been leveled at them. When considering the shortcomings of counterfactual accounts of causation, it is most important to attend to the general structure that all counterfactual theories have in common rather than picking on the details of one particular formulation.

1. Counterfactual accounts of causation are in several important respects insufficiently systematic. For starters, how are we supposed to know what the truth values of the

relevant counterfactuals are? In the examples I have presented, I tried to appeal to the intuitive plausibility of the counterfactuals, but on what basis is any judgment of a counterfactual justified? Are the counterfactual conditionals being used to settle questions about causation based on anything more than offhand opinion?

To be sure, no one can gather empirical evidence about something that does not exist. To the extent that we can say anything reasonable about non-actual possibilities, it is because our talk of non-actual scenarios conveys information about the actual world. For concreteness, we can examine how one prominent scheme for evaluating counterfactual conditionals, the forking account, applies to an unremarkable instance of causation. Let's imagine that a student brings home a canister of ice cream, forgets to place it in the freezer, leaves it on the table, and it melts. We want to examine whether leaving the ice cream on the table was one of the causes of the ice cream's melting. According to the forking account, to evaluate "If the ice cream had not been left on the table, it would not have melted," we hypothetically go back to sometime shortly before the ice cream was left on the table, and we then imagine an alternate history forking off from the actual history. It first unfolds by having the ice cream not being left on the table, presumably by the student putting it in the freezer, and second by having all other events proceed normally according to the usual laws of nature operating on the counterfactual state of affairs. Unless there is some reason to think the freezer would not have operated properly, we can conclude that the ice cream would not have melted. And that vindicates our common sense judgment that leaving the ice cream on the table was a cause of its melting. In this case, the truth of the counterfactual encodes information about (1) the state of the actual world at the time the student put the ice cream on the table – that the freezer was not broken, that the electricity supply was operating normally, etc. – and about (2) the laws of nature.

The ice cream example suggests that we can make sense of a general procedure for evaluating the counterfactuals relevant to causal claims, and that it matches our common sense judgments about causation. But is it adequate more generally? One example suggesting it does not always match our common sense judgments is Morgenbesser's coin:[2] Assume the laws of nature have a pervasive fundamental chanciness so that the outcomes of coin flips are never determined by pre-existing microscopic conditions. Now imagine a scenario in which Marcy calls out her guess that the next coin flip will land 'heads', the coin is flipped fairly by someone else, and the coin lands 'tails'. In this scenario, Marcy lost the coin flip. Furthermore, if you survey people, you will find that they tend to think that if Marcy had called 'tails', she would have won. Yet, according to the forking account, there is no fact of the matter about whether she would have won had she bet 'tails' because there is no fact of the matter about how the fundamentally chancy coin flip would have landed in the counterfactual history. What might be going on here is that people's knowledge about causation – that calling out a guess at the outcome does not have any effect on the probability of the outcome – is driving their judgment that the coin flip would have turned out the same if Marcy had said 'tails'. This suggests that our judgments about counterfactuals are influenced by our judgments about causation, so that we cannot expect to analyze causation purely in terms of our instinctive judgments about the truth values of counterfactuals.

2.   Most of the literature on counterfactual accounts of causation quantifies counterfactual dependence in terms of the *truth values* of counterfactual conditionals, which are understood to have a binary value: true or false. This makes it difficult for this literature to characterize degrees of difference-making. Furthermore, it is commonly assumed that the relevant counterfactuals obey many of the axioms identified in Lewis's (1973b) book on the implicit logic of counterfactual conditionals as they occur in English. But why would we ever expect rules governing the dependence of effects on their causes to adhere to the structures of a natural language like English? For just one example, recall that in Lewis's account, it is automatically true that "If $O(c_i)$ were true, then $O(e)$ would have been true," whenever c_i and e occur. In particular, it is true even when c_i and e are on opposite sides of the universe and even when e occurs billions of years before c_i.

Let's construct a specific counterexample by imagining a scenario where some c_i occurred, followed by some unrelated event e that happened far away from c_i and was fundamentally very probable (but not determined) at the time c_i occurred. The fact that both events occurred implies that if c_i had occurred, then e would have occurred. The fact that e was very probable implies the falsity of "If c_i had not occurred (and nature had proceeded lawfully thereafter), then e would not have occurred." In other words, event e probably would have occurred even if c_i had not. We thus have a case here where the counterfactual account of causation implies that c_i is a cause of e, which appears to be the wrong verdict given that the two events are unrelated by any physical interaction.

As usual, a wide variety of counterexamples have provoked an extensive back-and-forth among scholars, largely over how to fine-tune the forking account of counterfactuals and how to tweak the counterfactual logic to secure better agreement between people's common sense judgments about causation and the truth values of relevant counterfactual conditionals. But the more astute observation is that it should not be remotely surprising that a bunch of adjustments are required in order to shoehorn a theory of causal dependence among events into a counterfactual logic whose original purpose was to explain people's judgments about logical relations among counterfactual statements. This suggests we should look for a measure of difference-making that is less beholden to the accidents of human language.

3. According to the rules of the game, the goal for a theory of causation is to match common sense judgments about which events were the causes of e across a range of real or imagined scenarios. When playing this game, advocates for counterfactual theories of causation struggle with scenarios involving redundant causes.

Redundant causation occurs when there is a backup cause or multiple causes in position to bring about the effect if one of the potential causes fails. It comes in several varieties. We have already discussed one example of the form of redundant causation known as preemption. The production of the leak in the canteen, c_2, was a cause of e, and the backup cause, the poisoning, c_1, was not a cause of e. Because c_1 was going to cause e except for the interference caused by c_2, we say that c_2 preempted c_1's causation of e and that c_1 was not a cause of e.

A form of redundant causation I mentioned in chapter 1 is overdetermination, where multiple causes are responsible for the effect occurring. In cases of symmetric overdetermination, the causes are the same in all relevant respects, such as two spikes simultaneously bursting a tire when either one working alone would have been sufficient. In cases of asymmetric overdetermination, there are differences among the causes that motivate us to distribute causal responsibility unevenly. For example, imagine a large truck and a police car speeding through the street market in a classic chase scene. The truck slams into a fruit stand, mostly destroying it, followed by the police car flattening what remained. A natural judgment is that the truck and police car destroyed the fruit stand even though the stand was beyond repair by the time the police car finished it off.

The difference between preemption and overdetermination consists in whether the backup was also a cause. The poisoning was a backup that was not a cause of death, and it counts as preempted. Each spike (in the pair that burst the tire) was a backup to the other, but each one was a cause by itself. Thus, each spiking of the tire was an overdetermining cause.

The problem posed by redundant causation is that when a potential cause c_1 has a backup c_2, the effect e generally does not causally depend on c_1. That is what it means for c_2 to be a backup: c_2 would have caused e if c_1 had failed. So, unless fixes are imposed, counterfactual accounts of causation will wrongly judge that the main cause was not a cause at all.

We have already seen two theoretical devices used to handle cases of preemption. (1) We characterized the effect with moderate fragility. We needed e to be not so fragile as to make virtually every event a cause of e, yet to be fragile enough so that the traveler's death does not count as a successful poisoning. (2) We needed causation to obtain not only for causal dependencies but also for chains of causal dependence.

Both requirements are questionable. Regarding (1), there appears to be no independent reason to believe there is any fact of the matter about how fragile an event is. That is, events are realized by nature in full detail, and it is merely a matter of our choice about how much to fuzz the details in our representation of them. Regarding (2), the principle that chains of causal dependence result in causation is tantamount to the claim that causation is transitive. Causation is said to be transitive whenever it holds as a matter of general principle that *A* is a cause of *C* whenever *A* is a cause of some *B* that is a cause of *C*. Transitivity has been challenged by some concrete counterexamples (Maslen 2004). For example, potassium salt is thrown in a fire, causing a purple flame, and in an unrelated incident, Elvis sticks his hand in the purple flame for too long and receives a burn for his effort. Intuitively, the potassium was not a cause of Elvis's burn. The problem is that once transitivity is invoked to explain why the production of the leak in the canteen was a cause, it generates instances of causation too easily. If the counterfactual account were to ignore causal chains by simply equating causation with a direct relation of causal dependence, it would produce the correct result: that the potassium salt was not a cause of Elvis's burn.

A common strategy is to invoke a more sophisticated evaluation of the relevant counterfactuals. A number of philosophers[3] have argued that causation is contrastive, meaning that it does not consist of a binary cause–effect relation, but that causal relations hold relative to hypothetical or counterfactual contrasts. The potassium caused the flame to be purple *rather than yellow*, but what caused Elvis's burn was that there was a flame *rather than no flame* at all. Because the contrasts characterizing the intermediate event do not match, application of the transitivity principle is inappropriate and the counterexample fails. The downside to this resolution is that one now needs to go back and revise the model of counterfactual dependence to incorporate the contrast-sensitive counterfactual conditionals.

In any case, there are other forms of redundant causation that serve as counterexamples to the most straightforward counterfactual accounts. The standard remedy used to address preemption is to take account of intermediary events through a chain of causal dependence, as evident in the example of the desert traveler. Yet there are counterexamples to similar cases that are unaffected by intermediate events. In an adaptation of a fanciful example (Schaffer 2000), the silver wizard casts a spell that is 50 percent effective, and if successful turns the prince and the queen into frogs at midnight. The golden wizard casts a spell that is 50 percent effective, and if successful turns the prince and the king into frogs at midnight. The operative laws of magic in this scenario ensure that the activation of the spells influence nothing until midnight. As it turns out, the prince and the king turn into frogs, but the queen doesn't. From this information alone, one can deduce that the golden wizard's spell was effective, and that the silver wizard's spell was not a cause of any enfrogment. This case of **overlapping causation** shows that without any intermediary events, the specific details of how the overall effect was realized are sufficient for us to determine that the silver wizard's spell was not a cause.

I have just tried to give you a taste of the kinds of debates that are currently popular in philosophical journals. There is a vast literature full of counterexamples, tweaks to the counterfactual approach, and counterexamples to the tweaks. Whole careers have been made working through the vast space of possibilities.

Practice Essays

At this stage, you should work through some examples on your own. Here are two to think about.

Consider the following definition of causation by omission introduced by Helen Beebee (2004, p. 294). Discuss how well it fares at matching common sense judgments.

> The nonoccurrence of an event of type A caused event b if and only if, had an A-type event occurred, b would not have occurred.

The following puzzle concerning symmetrical overdetermination was stated by L. A. Paul (2009). Attempt to state and defend the resolution that seems best to you. It concerns an example where each of two independent events, c_1 and c_2, instantiates a rock striking a window simultaneously with the other. c_1 and c_2 are for all purposes exactly alike, and together they cause the effect e, the breaking of a window. Either by itself would have caused the very same kind of damage to the window. Paul uses "counterfactually depends" for what was earlier "causally depends," and I have altered the variables to maintain consistency.

> e does not counterfactually depend on c_2 because c_1 also causes it. Likewise, e does not counterfactually depend on c_1 because c_2 also causes it. The defender of counterfactual analyses seems to be forced to fall back on one of two options: neither c_1 nor c_2 caused e, for e is counterfactually dependent on neither of them, or the [composition] of c_1 and c_2 caused e, for e is counterfactually dependent on this [composite event].
>
> Holding that neither c_1 nor c_2 is a cause of e is unconvincing. e was caused, and c_1 and c_2 each seem to have caused it. How can it make sense to say that neither c_1 nor c_2 is a cause of e? The latter option is more appealing: the sum of c_1 and c_2 caused e. But note that this won't get the counterfactual analyst as much as might seem. Taking the [composition] of c_1 and c_2 as the cause does not mean that we are taking c_1 as a cause and c_2 as a cause: instead, the [composite event] $c_1 + c_2$ is a cause while neither event alone is.
>
> This result is bizarre. How can the [composite event] $c_1 + c_2$ be a cause of e while neither c_1 nor c_2 alone is a cause, joint or otherwise?

Summary

Difference-making is arguably an essential component of causation, but scholars are divided about how best to quantify difference-making and how it relates to other aspects of causation such as production and probability-raising. At their best, difference-making models of causation are praiseworthy for spelling out how causes affect.

I have tried to convey the most common way difference-making has been incorporated into a theory of causation, a model of causation among events that equates causation with chains of causal (and thus counterfactual) dependence. This particular implementation is subject to general doubts: We don't have an independent grip on the relevant counterfactuals, they are too clumsily characterized using the logic of natural language counterfactuals, and our somewhat capricious methods of individuating events makes causation depend too much on us. The implementation is also subject to more specific doubts about how to categorize scenarios involving redundant causation.

Questions

Q: I found it a bit weird that you were discussing magic spells. I get that wizards are more interesting than flipping coins, but what does it matter how we classify causes that have no real-world application?

A: If you survey philosophers, you are going to find many who say it does not matter whether we use magic-based examples because the ultimate goal is to identify features of our *concept* of causation. Our concept of causation, as everyone agrees, applies to more than just the cases of causation that we find in the actual world. I must say that I do not agree with that answer, but I do think an alternative justification is available. So far as I can tell, the purpose of these far-fetched examples is to highlight when a theory of causation is not adequately adapted to the underlying laws.

It is reasonable to require the metaphysics of causation and the causal laws to play nicely together because, broadly speaking, they both have the job of explaining why nature evolves as it does. In some cases, our judgments of causation need to bend to what the laws dictate. If we really believe it is a consequence of the fundamental laws that particle decay is generally a fundamentally chancy phenomenon, then we should also believe of some particular decay event that there was nothing that caused the particle to decay precisely when and how it did. In other cases, our guesses at the laws need to be adjusted to fit with observed causal regularities. If we really believe the sun causes starlight to bend, then we need to reject any theory of fundamental physics that says the position of the sun never plays a role in the motion of starlight.

Relating this back to wizardry, if we are confident that the fundamental laws dictate that the silver wizard's spell must either simultaneously enfrog both the prince and queen or have no effect whatsoever, then we ought to judge that the silver wizard's spell was not a cause of the prince turning into a frog when the queen was unaffected. Essentially, the purpose of the magic example here is to explore laws that are somewhat different from the actual laws (by exerting influence that hops into the future rather than proceeding continuously) in order to make sure that the devices we have chosen to identify redundant non-causes are robust enough to apply to a reasonable range of possible laws.

Q: Where did you get that quotation at the beginning?

A: It is from a novel I read five or six years ago. Its author has not been born yet, but look for it in the future.

Further Reading

The literature on counterfactual theories of causation is large but also largely accessible. An article that touches on its relation to production is Alyssa Ney's (2009) "Physical Causation and Difference-Making." An older review of some of the standard philosophical literature on counterfactuals is Dorothy Edgington's (1995) "On Conditionals."

5
Determination

"Causes," it is said, "*make* their effects happen." One traditional way of understanding what it is to *make* an effect happen is for the cause to *determine* that the effect will occur. The basic idea is that the occurrence of some collection of events somehow ensures that an effect of some prescribed character will also occur. The nature of this guarantee and how it can be parlayed into an account of causation is our subject for this chapter.

Here is a definition of determination:

> An event c **determines** an event e just in case the laws of nature together with the occurrence of c suffice for the occurrence of e. When c determines e, we say there is a determination relation holding from c to e.

Determination captures the idea that the guarantee is provided by a *law of nature*. Philosophers have long puzzled over what precisely a law of nature is, but fortunately we can bracket much of the controversy concerning laws by focusing on a few traditional examples of deterministic laws.

According to one modern formulation of classical physics, for instance, fundamental reality can be characterized as having two kinds of components:

1. There is a complete state for every moment in the history of the universe. Each state comprises the location, mass, and speed of every particle at a single moment.
2. There is a deterministic dynamical law. A dynamical law specifies how a given state develops through time (toward the future and the past). When it specifies exactly one future (and one past) for a generic state, we say it is deterministic. When it allows for more than one future and specifies probabilities for these possible futures, we say it is fundamentally chancy.

In the words of William James, deterministic dynamical laws imply

> that those parts of the universe already laid down absolutely appoint and decree what the other parts shall be. The future has no ambiguous possibilities hidden within its womb: the part we call the present is only compatible with one totality. Any other future complement than the one fixed from eternity is impossible. (1897, para. 6)

When trying to understand the formal definition of 'determination' at a deeper level, I find it helpful to distinguish *determination* from *determinism*. **Determinism** is the proposition that *any* state of the world permitted by the laws of nature determines what would happen in the world at all other times. Determination relations can exist without determinism holding. For illustration, imagine our universe includes a single fundamentally chancy event in the far distant future but that everything before then is determined by previous events. In that case, everything around us is determined, but *determinism* does not hold.

Another instructive example is Norton's dome. John Norton (2008) proved that according to the laws of classical physics, a perfectly point-sized particle placed on top of an appropriately shaped dome might remain motionless for a minute or an hour or a year and then spontaneously slide off the dome in some undetermined direction without anything knocking it off the top. Norton's dome demonstrates that classical physics violates determinism because the permitted arrangement fails to determine when or in what direction the particle will slide off. However, classical physics is nonetheless capable of generating determination relations because Norton's proof requires the very peak of the dome to be fundamentally solid with a distinctive shape. Norton's dome does not pronounce on whether the *actual future* is determined by the actual present even if we pretend that classical physics governs our world, for the actual world does not include any such domes.

Another idea to contrast with determination is predictability. The French astronomer and mathematician Pierre-Simon Laplace (1820, p. 4) described deterministic dynamical laws using the following metaphor:

> An intelligence knowing all the forces acting in nature at a given instant, as well as the momentary positions of all things in the universe, would be able to comprehend in one single formula the motions of the largest bodies as well as the lightest atoms, provided that its intellect were sufficiently powerful to subject all data to analysis; to it, nothing would be uncertain, the future as well as the past would be present to its eyes.

For the purposes of studying causation, we need to set aside the question of how much can be deduced from our knowledge of the present state of the world because it raises too many questions about the cognitive powers of this fictitious "intelligence." Even in very simple examples, like three particles interacting gravitationally, it is mathematically impossible to solve the equations that imply their future locations; one can only approximate their positions with ever-greater accuracy. Despite our inability to ascertain the exact future in this case, the laws of nature permit only one possible future (given present conditions). *Determination* concerns the behavior of the *world*; *predictability* concerns *idealized knowledge* of this behavior, which is usually more limited.

There are more subtleties one can dig into concerning determination, but let's move on. What does determination have to do with causation? Several philosophers have proposed analyzing causation in terms of determination. That is, they accept determination relations as relatively unproblematic and attempt to define causal relations in terms of determination. Let's look at some of the history of this idea.

History of Causation as Determination

Recall that Hume said our concept of causation incorporates the idea of a necessary connection: that there is something in the cause that *necessitates* the effect. The modern way to understand 'necessity' is in terms of logical or mathematical implication. Nowadays, we accept that the redness of an apple necessitates that the apple is colored, and we agree with Hume that the movement of one billiard ball into another does not necessitate that the second will move because we can consistently imagine that it remains at rest. At best, a cause determines its effect rather than necessitating it. A charitable way to interpret talk of events necessitating each other is to construe 'necessitation' as determination.

Another figure, John Stuart Mill, is famous for his political tract *On Liberty*, but he also wrote a large volume (1843) entitled *A System of Logic*, a portion of which discusses causal relationships. Let's study an extended quotation from Mill. (His language is somewhat dated, so take note that an antecedent is "that which goes before," a consequent is "that which follows," and a concurrence is a "running together.")

> We may define, therefore, the cause of a phenomenon, to be the antecedent, or the concurrence of antecedents, on which it is invariably and unconditionally consequent.
>
> It is seldom, if ever, between a consequent and a single antecedent, that this invariable sequence subsists. It is usually between a consequent and the sum of several antecedents; the concurrence of all of them being requisite to produce, that is, to be certain of being followed by, the consequent. In such cases it is very common to single out one only of the antecedents under the denomination of Cause, calling the others merely Conditions. Thus, if a person eats of a particular dish, and dies in consequence, that is, would not have died if he had not eaten of it, people would be apt to say that eating of that dish was the cause of his death. There needs not, however, be any invariable connection between eating of the dish and death; but there certainly is, among the circumstances which took place, some combination or other on which death is invariably consequent: as, for instance, the act of eating of the dish, combined with a particular bodily constitution, a

particular state of present health, and perhaps even a certain state of the atmosphere; the whole of which circumstances perhaps constituted in this particular case the *conditions* of the phenomenon, or, in other words, the set of antecedents which determined it, and but for which it would not have happened. The real Cause, is the whole of these antecedents; and we have, philosophically speaking, no right to give the name of cause to one of them, exclusively of the others. What, in the case we have supposed, disguises the incorrectness of the expression, is this: that the various conditions, except the single one of eating the food, were not *events* (that is, instantaneous changes, or successions of instantaneous changes) but *states*, possessing more or less of permanency; and might therefore have preceded the effect by an indefinite length of duration, for want of the event which was requisite to complete the required concurrence of conditions: while as soon as that event, eating the food, occurs, no other cause is waited for, but the effect begins immediately to take place: and hence the appearance is presented of a more immediate and close connection between the effect and that one antecedent, than between the effect and the remaining conditions. But though we may think proper to give the name of cause to that one condition, the fulfillment of which completes the tale, and brings about the effect without further delay; this condition has really no closer relation to the effect than any of the other conditions has. All the conditions were equally indispensable to the production of the consequent; and the statement of the cause is incomplete, unless in some shape or other we introduce them all. A man takes mercury, goes out-of-doors, and catches cold. We say, perhaps, that the cause of his taking cold was exposure to the air. It is clear, however, that his having taken mercury may have been a necessary condition of his catching cold; and though it might consist with usage to say that the cause of his attack was exposure to the air, to be accurate we ought to say that the cause was exposure to the air while under the effect of mercury.

If there be any meaning which confessedly belongs to the term necessity, it is unconditionalness. That which is necessary, that which must be, means that which will be, whatever supposition we may make in regard to all other things. (1930 [1843], pp. 237–8)

There is a lot of good philosophy here. Let me just highlight a few of his statements for emphasis.

Mill defines the cause of e to be the "concurrence of antecedents" that makes e "invariably and unconditionally consequent." So three conditions are necessary for an instance c of type C to cause an instance e of type E:

- c must precede e in time.
- Cs must always be followed by Es.
- It must be that Cs would be followed by Es no matter what other conditions are hypothetically imposed.

If all three of these conditions hold, then c is the cause of e.

Note that Mill defines "the" cause of a phenomenon, which carries a connotation that an effect has only one real cause. According to just about any deterministic theory, however, there exist multiple determining causes at different (and typically all) previous times. An effect e is determined by everything that happened one second ago, and by everything that happened two seconds ago, and by everything that happened three seconds ago, and so on. Perhaps Mill could be interpreted as identifying the real cause of e with the conglomeration of all such determining conditions.

Note also that Mill's definition is similar to the regularity view of causation we discussed earlier. The main difference is Mill's additional requirement that the connection between cause and effect be unconditional. Mill did not specify precisely what he meant by 'unconditional', but the very last sentence I quoted seems to indicate that he thinks about it in the following way. Suppose you are considering a "concurrence of antecedents" c as a candidate for being a full cause of some e. If c is the real cause, according to Mill, not only does c determine e, but you should be able to add hypothetically to c any other conditions at any other places or times to define bigger concurrences of antecedents $c_1, c_2, \ldots$, and all of these bigger concurrences will also determine e. Given the occurrence of c, nothing can be added to stop e from happening. This unconditionality requirement, we should recognize, goes a bit against the motivating idea for the regularity view, because unconditionality appears to be equivalent to the requirement that there be a strict law that ensures e happens when c happens.

The final example I want to mention in this scandalously brief history of determination-based theories of causation comes from a 1973 book by J. L. Mackie, *The Cement of the Universe*. Mackie's work is essential reading for students of causation, and there are a hundred ideas in his book that deserve investigation. But in order to cut to the chase, I will just summarize his inus account of causation because it is a standard point of reference.

Mackie presents a refinement of Mill's account using variables that range over "conditions," including events like a match being struck, S, enabling conditions like the presence of oxygen, O, and negative conditions like the absence of wind, $\underline{W}$. The conjunction of these conditions, S & O & $\underline{W}$, is a full cause that determines the lighting of the match, E. Real life is more complicated, so that a full cause is typically represented by a very long conjunction of such variables, but let's keep it simple.

Building on Mill's further observation that an effect typically could have been caused by other assemblages of conditions, Mackie points out that a causal regularity can take the form of a disjunction of conjunctions. For example, E occurs just in case S & O & $\underline{W}$ or L & O & $\underline{M}$ or . . . , where L stands for the presence of a laser beam pointed at the matchstick and $\underline{M}$ stands for the lack of a mirror in the path of the laser. Again, in real life, the list of 'or's will be very long. Such is the nature of a real causal regularity.

Mackie then characterizes a partial cause of E as one of the conditions represented by these variables. He calls them 'inus conditions' for E. An inus is "an insufficient but necessary part of an unnecessary but sufficient" condition for E. Each full cause in the causal regularity is "an unnecessary but sufficient condition" for E: sufficient because it determines E and unnecessary because other possible full causes could have brought about E instead. Each partial cause is an "insufficient but necessary" part of a full cause: insufficient because the partial cause by itself does not determine E and necessary because if it were not present, its full cause would not be full enough to determine E. All of this is just a formalization of the idea that partial causes are conditions that work together to determine an effect.

The upshot of this history is that determination accounts characterize full causes as conditions determining the effect and partial causes as their essential parts.

Advantages

1. The most promising feature of determination accounts of causation is that they match up pretty well with historically prominent physical theories that gesture toward a complete theory of fundamental reality. Newton's theory of gravity and Einstein's special and general theories of relativity use determination relations to bind events together causally. If we suspect that physics is relatively well positioned to give us a rich and detailed account of how the universe behaves fundamentally, we should take note that determination plays a prominent role in such theories.

2. Determination helps to provide some of the desired features of a productive conception of causation. Recall that production is ordinarily conceived as a continuous process where each stage of production brings about later stages. Determination has built-in transitivity to ensure that if stage 1 produces stage 2 (by determining it) and stage 2 produces stage 3 (by determining it) then stage 1 will produce stage 3. And all prominent deterministic theories implement their determination relations in a continuous way so that no determination relations hop through time. So, if the kinds of determination relations from physics exist, they behave somewhat like a causal production.

Challenges

There are several recognized problems with determination-based theories of causation.

1. For all we know, the world might incorporate a fair amount of fundamental chanciness. If so, there will not be enough determination relations for the theory to apply to

prototypical examples of causation. That would knock down any claim that causation requires determination.

Even if our world happens to be replete with determination relations, the dependency on determination is still a deficiency. Because it is difficult to establish whether the actual world incorporates fundamental chanciness, determination accounts of causation are reliant on a speculative hypothesis. Imagine a fundamental law dictating that events of type C have a 99.999 . . . 9 percent chance of being followed by events of type E, where I have omitted a million 9s. For almost all practical purposes, it won't matter that this chance is not exactly 100 percent. If you observe a C, you will be able to predict reliably that its corresponding E will occur. If you are able to control whether a C occurs, you will be able to control whether its E occurs. Yet according to a determination account, Cs do not cause Es. This mismatch between the conceptual role played by 'causation' and the causation attributed by the determination account reveals that the determination account does not adequately track what is important about causation.

2. Causation appears to be directed only toward the future, yet the kinds of deterministic laws that appear in physics almost always bestow at least some determination relations that go toward the past as well. This raises the thorny question of what is responsible for the direction of causation. One possibility is that our world includes a fundamental causal direction, but many contemporary experts are hesitant to accept the fundamentality of causal direction, primarily because of worries about whether we could gather any scientific evidence for a fundamental direction and worries about how well it integrates with other "arrows of time."

If the direction of causation is not fundamental, then determination accounts will need to be supplemented. Given the prominent role of causation's future-directedness, one might reasonably wonder whether determination could still play a prominent role in the account once the resources to explain causal directedness have been successfully incorporated.

3. Historically prominent determination accounts are illustrated using scenarios that involve determination relations among collections of macroscopic conditions. In Mill's example, the diner's death was determined by the dish being

eaten, his bodily constitution, his present health, the atmosphere, and so on. Yet all prominent deterministic theories in the history of physics require the determining causes to include absolutely every last microphysical detail throughout a vast volume of space. Physicists' preferred dynamical laws imply that determination relations virtually never exist among human-scale antecedents like meals and humans and the atmosphere. As a result, determination accounts fail to match up with uncontroversial truths about causation in two ways.

Regarding singular causation, determination accounts are overly permissive. The full cause of the diner's death includes the arrangement of starfish on the bottom of the ocean a thousand years ago, the precise pattern of radio static in the atmosphere last year, etc. All such happenings are among the causes of the diner's death. What's more, they are all equally causes. The historical layout of starfish is just as much an inus condition as the germs in the toxic dish insofar as the physical development of the universe is concerned. Unless determination accounts can be supplemented with some additional resources, they will render just about everything a cause of everything else, and that would fail to make sense of how we are often able to identify a limited number of *distinguished* causes.

Regarding general causation, determination accounts are not permissive enough. It was a major medical breakthrough for humans to learn that germs cause illness. But there is no general determination relation between germs and illness. Not all illnesses are preceded by corresponding germs, and not all germs lead to illness. Unless determination accounts can be supplemented with some additional resources, they will wrongly judge that the relation between germs and illness is not causal.

4. Determination accounts struggle to account for the difference-making aspects of causation. Consider, for example, that determination accounts do not attribute causation in degrees. Yet many of our measurements of causation attribute degrees of causal power or causal responsibility to objects. Imagine a spring scale that measures 0.7 kg bananas and then measures 1.0 kg when mangoes are added. The bunch of bananas is responsible for 70 percent of the displacement of the scale, and the mangoes are responsible for 30 percent.

How can a determination theory account for this, especially given the lesson that both the mangoes and bananas are equally needed to determine that the scale shows 1.0 kg?

Questions

Q: It sounds like these theories must be pretty bad if they cannot handle chanciness because we already know from quantum mechanics that the world is not deterministic. Am I right?

A: Two quickies: First, no one knows whether the actual world is deterministic, and the vast amount of evidence scientists have accumulated in favor of quantum mechanics has not helped to decide the issue one way or the other. Some versions of quantum mechanics are fundamentally chancy while others are deterministic.

Second, it is certainly a big problem for determination-based theories of causation that they falter in scenarios incorporating fundamental chanciness. After all, we seem to know from experience and science that there are reliable causal relations in the world, but the determination accounts suggest that the existence of causation should be hard to detect, for it is difficult to ascertain whether the world is fundamentally chancy or whether instead the events of our world are cemented together by relations of determination.

The next step in thinking about this problem is to assess whether the determination accounts can be modified or extended to accommodate chanciness without undercutting their previously cited advantages. That might be a big project, but perhaps there is reason for hope in the recognition that regardless of what we think about the fundamental nature of causation, we need to be able to make sense of how the world can behave in a chancy way at the human scale. We need some reasonable explanation of how the chanciness of dice and cards and coin flips can coexist with our ignorance of whether the world is fundamentally chancy. Maybe there is a way to structure a theory of causation to bracket this issue so that the details of the explanation can be left to others and so that our concerns about the nature of causation do not depend on the details.

Q: How are determination and counterfactual dependence related?

A: I know of two different answers that appear in the literature on causation. First, some background: Both Hume and Mill use language that suggests to modern ears that they thought of counterfactual dependence and necessitation as interchangeable.

Have another look at the quotation from Mill, where he says, "the set of antecedents which determined [the effect], and but for which [the effect] would not have happened." The point here is that he seems to be claiming that if the full concurrence of antecedents had not occurred, the effect would not have occurred. And that is an attribution of counterfactual (or causal) dependence.

Similarly, David Hume gave two alternative definitions of causation in his *An Enquiry Concerning Human Understanding*:

> We may define a cause to be *an object, followed by another, and where all the objects similar to the first are followed by objects similar to the second*. Or in other words *where, if the first objects had not been, the second never had existed*. (1748, sec. VII)

You should recognize Hume's first definition here as a version of the regularity view described in chapter 2. His suggestion that the first and second definitions are interchangeable is curious. The first definition talks about scenarios that *actually* occur. It defines causes as things of a certain kind that are, in the *actual* world, always followed by things of another kind. The second defines causation in terms of relations between non-actual occurrences. It defines causes in terms of what *would* have happened if the world had been different. How can such seemingly different concepts express the same definition?

I think that it helps here to examine Nelson Goodman's (1947) work on counterfactual conditionals. Let's work through an example. Someone strikes a match and it lights. We want to account for the apparent fact that what caused the match to light was striking it. To do so, we consider whether the match would have lit if it had not been struck. To do this, we consider the state of the world at a time roughly when the match was struck, and use truths about what is going on then to determine the truth value of "If the match had not been struck, it would not have lit." Intuitively, we think this statement is true, and Goodman's analysis of counterfactuals backs this up. Roughly speaking, for Goodman, a counterfactual is true when there is a set of true statements S (describing existing conditions), such that S conjoined with A logically implies the consequent, C. S is not allowed to include any statements that contradict the assumption of A. In Goodman's example, A is "The match was not struck," C is "The match remains unlit" and S includes truths like "The match was dry," "There was oxygen present," "There is a person holding the match." It appears Goodman thought that in this scenario, if there were deterministic laws L, then S could encompass enough true statements about what was going on at time t for $A \& S \& L$ to entail C and thereby vindicate our judgment that striking the match caused it to light.

In Goodman's theory, deterministic laws are normally required for the propositions about the counterfactual situation at time t, namely $A \& S$, to entail truths about what happens later. In this way, determination relations establish which counterfactual statements are true, which in turn establish which statements about causation are true. So we can now give one answer to your original question, which was, "How are determination and counterfactual dependence related?" Following Goodman's approach to counterfactuals, a deterministic law is needed for counterfactual dependence. The deterministic law is basic, and counterfactual conditionals are just our conventional way of expressing what the law implies about any postulated situation, actual or non-actual.

Because Goodman's approach to counterfactuals is unpopular and because we do not know whether the actual world has deterministic laws, it is better to take a broader view of how the theories we have discussed can relate to counterfactuals.

Unfortunately, the mainstream view that counterfactuals should be understood in light of standard counterfactual logics does not lend itself to a simple statement about how they relate to determination-based theories. So I think we would need to step up our discussion to an advanced level to get an adequate answer. Let me instead just offer you one nugget of information that will help you to start looking into this yourself. Have a look at the brief discussion in Lewis's (1973a) article "Causation," where he claims that his counterfactual theory of causation is able to encompass determination relations as a special case.

Finally, this question about determination and counterfactuals is a good one for us to end on because it relates to a distinction I mentioned in chapter 1: production vs. difference-making. Accounts of causation based on determination are geared more toward a productive conception of causation. (Peek back at the quotation from Mill to find him mentioning this.) Counterfactual accounts of causation are geared toward a difference-making conception. Because causation seems to involve both production and difference-making, this raises the question to aspiring philosophers of whether it is better to capture the productive aspects of causation using the resources of a difference-making conception, or the other way around. Or is the tension between the two aspects irreconcilable? That would be an excellent question to answer.

Further Reading

I strongly recommend reading Mackie's (1973) *The Cement of the Universe*. A modern formulation of Mackie's basic idea can be found in Michael Strevens's (2007) "Mackie Remixed" and in my (2013) book.

6
Probability-Raising

Much of the distant history of thought concerning causation attended to the idea that causes are singular events that in some sense *necessitate* their effects. But as we discussed in the previous chapter, one glaring deficiency of traditional determination accounts of causation is their inability to handle chancy causal relations. In this chapter, we are going to flip the script and look at one philosophical approach that tries to fashion an account of causation using probabilistic relations among events. The motivating idea is that when there is a causal regularity going from Cs to Es, an instance of E is more likely to occur when some instance of C has occurred than when everything is the same except that no instance of C has occurred.

It is not difficult to see why the incorporation of probability is important. First, it is hard to discern whether the world incorporates fundamental chanciness rather than abundant relations of determination. On the one hand, it is usually easy to alter a deterministic model of the universe by inserting a tiny bit of chanciness whose effects will be nearly impossible to discern. On the other hand, arguments that our world must contain fundamental chanciness have traditionally fared very poorly. Famously, quantum mechanics has been alleged to require fundamental chanciness, but no good supporting arguments have yet been found. Quite generally, it is difficult to establish that a scientific theory with fundamental chanciness cannot be replaced by an equally good deterministic theory.

Despite our ignorance about how nature operates fundamentally, we can be extremely confident that the world contains many causal relationships. This suggests that causation should be understood so that its existence is insensitive to how much determination exists. A good way to do this is to allow causes to make their effects have a certain probability of occurring rather than simply making their effects occur.

Second, there is no practical difference between *c*'s making *e*'s occurrence *very nearly* certain and *c*'s making *e*'s occurrence *absolutely* certain. Suppose flipping a certain switch reliably activates its attached alarm using a simple mechanism that has a minuscule chance of failure. When an engineer flips the switch one day and the alarm activates as usual, it would be hard to deny that flipping the switch *caused* the alarm to activate, even though it did not *determine* the alarm's activation. If we insist that causes determine their effects, though, we will wrongly judge that it was not a cause.

Probability-Raising Accounts of Causation

The development of theories of causation based on probability-raising follows a path through Hans Reichenbach (1956), I. J. Good (1961, 1962), Patrick Suppes (1970), Nancy Cartwright (1979), and Ellery Eells (1991), up to the more recent causal modeling literature based on Bayesian networks, which we will encounter in chapter 7. There are differences among these accounts, especially different conceptions of probability, but all of the work from the authors listed here differ from another group of theories: counterfactual and productive accounts that incorporate chanciness. The distinctive feature that sets apart the theories known as 'probability-raising accounts' from other theories of causation that invoke probability is that probability-raising accounts define probabilistic difference-making in terms of (suitably idealized) statistical relationships found in the actual world, rather than using fundamental laws that specify chances governing how the world evolves.

My plan is to outline some preliminary concepts, and then to present a basic version of the main principles guiding probability-raising accounts. We can spend the rest of the chapter unpacking their presuppositions.

Probabilities

The intuitive motivation for the concept of probability is that it allows us to *quantify* possibilities on a scale from impossible to certain.

By consulting the relevant mathematics textbooks, you can find the standard conception of probability defined by the following three axioms,[1] plus some extra presuppositions like the stipulation that every probability has a determinate magnitude that can be represented by a single real number:

- Axiom 1 establishes that the smallest probability for any event type is zero.
- Axiom 2 establishes the convention that the complete space of all possibilities under consideration has probability one.
- Axiom 3 establishes the additive relationship between a collection of mutually exclusive event types and the single event type that comprises them all. For example, the probability that A or B or C will occur is equal to the probability that A will occur plus the probability that B will occur plus the probability that C will occur, assuming that A, B, and C are mutually exclusive in the sense that no single occurrence can instantiate more than one of them.

These axioms are the orthodox rules a quantity has to obey in order to count formally as a probability, though alternative axioms do exist.

To investigate how probabilities apply to the actual world is to tread into hotly disputed territory. Philosophers are naturally prone to befuddlement and contention on every topic, and the concept of probability is no exception. Unfortunately, much of the philosophical literature on probability adopts the awkward stance that there is a unique entity called 'probability' that admits of competing "interpretations." A better way to frame the issue, I think, is to think of a probability in general as any quantity governed by the Kolmogorov axioms (or some suitable alternative). Then a person can identify or characterize different quantities that possess this formal probabilistic structure. The various possible implementations of probability do not exclude each other.

In particular, a critical warning about these axioms is warranted. If you look at textbook treatments of probability, they will use the word 'event' in this set of definitions in place of 'event type', and what they mean by 'event' is an event type that is more abstract than the one we have considered so far. For example, an event in probability theory (really an event type) does not necessarily incorporate any information about the spatial or temporal relationships between possible occurrences, nor does it necessarily incorporate any information about laws of nature. It is a requirement of the standard framework of probability theory that one simply specify in advance the full space of possibilities one wishes to consider.

Probabilistic Relations

The conception of probability operative in probability-raising accounts of causation is based on observed statistical frequencies, adjusted to account for statistical noise. For example, it is uncontroversial that the probability of a standard cubic die landing with a number four faceup when tossed in a fair manner is 1 in 6. One good reason for thinking this is that dice have been rolled often and have displayed each face upward very nearly one-sixth of the time across a wide variety of conditions such as different people tossing the dice, different materials for the dice and surface, and so on.[2] Another good reason for thinking the probability is one-sixth is that we can examine a die to verify that it has a cubic symmetry and apply our knowledge of physics to ascertain whether the tossing conditions are sufficiently chaotic to make each outcome very nearly equally likely. In practice, scientists operate on the assumption that if numerous tests are performed, the observed frequencies will *nearly* match the probabilities where the nearness can be quantified. Yet, as any good student of probability knows, there is no guarantee that the distribution of outcomes from a chancy process will match the probabilities. In some special cases, we are allowed to maintain that the observed frequencies do not represent the "true" probabilistic relations.

For example, suppose we make a die out of the rare-earth element einsteinium and roll it exactly 1,000 times, and the outcome 'four' exhibits a frequency of only 1/10, and then the die is destroyed with no einsteinium die ever existing again. The prescription I have laid out tells us that the default value for the probability, P, of an einsteinium die producing a 'four' is 1/10. However, I do not think we should believe that P is 1/10. We should believe that P is 1/6 because we have a vast amount of data concerning dice generally, and it is not remotely plausible that there is something in the chemistry or physics of einsteinium to suggest that einsteinium in particular bestows a probability of 1/10 on the 'four' outcome. The most reasonable interpretation of the actual frequency of 1/10 is that it was a fluke.

To summarize, the concept of probability employed by probability-raising accounts of causation is one whose default magnitude is nearly the actual frequency of the designated outcome but can depart from the actual frequency in certain circumstances.

Putting all of this into practice, we can identify a probabilistic relation going from some event type C to an event type E as having a value equal to the actual frequency of C events that are followed by E events, modified by a fudge factor that takes into account additional information relevant to our expectations about future occurrences of Cs and Es, like symmetries, known bias in the sampling of the C-type events, and outcomes of similar chancy processes. The resulting value is the probability of E given C, abbreviated as $P(E \mid C)$.

The word 'given' has a technical meaning in probability theory. It does not mean that one postulates the existence of some hypothetical C and then derives the probability that E

would have in the imagined scenario. Rather, 'E given C' means the probability of E among those possibilities where C occurs. Translated into mathematics, the so-called **conditional probability**, $P(E \mid C)$, is by stipulation equal to $P(E \& C)/P(C)$ in cases where its magnitude is well defined. (It is not well defined when $P(C) = 0$ because that would involve dividing by zero.)

A philosophical consequence of the fact that probabilistic relations from C-type events to E-type events are quantified by conditional probabilities is that they do not incorporate any causal oomph. It is incorrect to think we are defining the probability of E given C to be "the probability that a C-event *makes* an E-event have." A probabilistic connection between C and E can be well defined and non-zero even when Cs and Es never interact. Probabilistic relations, as normally conceived, exist only by virtue of the historical layout of events. Although causation is understood in terms of E's being more likely when a C has occurred, such probability-raising does not imply that C *makes* E more likely in some productive sense of causation. In terms of a distinction drawn in chapter 1, probability-raising accounts attend only to the pattern-based aspects of causation, not the influence-based aspects.

That having been noted, one should recognize that it is the goal of probability-raising theories of causation to derive information about the causal relationship between C and E from the probabilistic relations. Advocates of these theories do identify causal relations as cases of probability-*raising*, and so misleadingly suggest production.

In Reichenbach's and Good's versions, causation between C and E is characterized in terms of conditional probabilities (including event types other than C and E) without needing any causal information as input. In effect, they propose to reduce causation to probabilistic relations. Cartwright, by contrast, argues that some preliminary causal assumptions are needed to extract causal information from probabilities. Even in non-reductive approaches like hers, though, probabilistic relations are intended to play an essential role in characterizing causal relations, causal tendencies, and causal powers.

Standard Accounts

Probability-raising accounts of causation attempt to specify rules that allow one to infer causal relations (perhaps in partnership with preliminary information about the operative causal structure). Probability-raising is defined using one of the following two rules, which are nearly equivalent:

(PR_1) C raises the probability of E exactly when $P(E \mid C) > P(E)$.
(PR_2) C raises the probability of E exactly when $P(E \mid C) > P(E \mid {\sim}C)$.

The first says that an E-type event is more likely to occur when a C-type event occurs. The second states that an E is more likely to occur when a C-type event occurs than when a C-type event does not occur. These are mathematically equivalent when the designated quantities are well defined.

An overly simplistic probability-raising theory of causation might then define causation as follows:

(PRC-Simplistic) C causes E exactly when C raises the probability of E.

Advocates of the probability-raising approach to causation do not advocate (PRC-Simplistic) mainly because of the *asymmetry of causation*, the possibility of *spurious correlations*, and *Simpson's paradox*. Let's go through these in order.

Asymmetry

The asymmetry of causation most relevant to probability-raising accounts can be specified as follows:

- There are many cases of asymmetric causation, where an event c is a cause of some effect e, and e is not a cause of c.

- There are no cases (or at least very few) of symmetric causation, where c is a cause of e and e is a cause of c.

The asymmetry problem for (PRC-Simplistic) is that it suggests there will be many cases of symmetric causation. Consider, for example, that telling a joke will raise the probability that the audience will laugh. No problem with that, but according to (PRC-Simplistic), it also appears to be true that the laughter of the audience will more likely be preceded by a joke than by pontification or rambling or silence. According to (PRC-Simplistic), that probabilistic relation means that the presence of laughter *raises* the probability of an earlier joke. You can construct many similar examples where probability-raising from a C to an E still exists after switching the places of E and C in the equation specified by (PRC-Simplistic).

The solution adopted by Good and Suppes is simply to stipulate that causes precede their effects. The solution adopted by Reichenbach (in his later work) is a more intricate maneuver that relies on his "principle of the common cause," which we will discuss shortly.

Spurious Correlations

The problem with probability-raising theories of causation posed by spurious correlations is illustrated by the following stock example. A low-pressure front arrives at the weather station; first, it causes the barometer's needle to point to a low value, and later it causes a rainstorm. Rainstorms are more likely when the barometer reading is low, but barometers do not appear to cause rainstorms. At least, if you grab the barometer needle and force it to a low reading, don't expect it to rain. Intuitively, the conditional probability of rain is higher, given a low barometer reading, because the low barometer reading is a good indicator that a low-pressure front is present, which does (causally) raise the probability of rain. The apparent problem with (PRC-Simplistic), just as we saw in the case of causal asymmetry, is that (PRC-Simplistic) does not distinguish evidential probability-raising from causal probability-raising. But in this case, one cannot fix the problem just by imposing a future-directedness on causation, for the barometer reading does precede the rainstorm. (Also, the barometer uncontroversially exerts *some* sort of influence on the precise character of the storm because the slight gravitational pull of the barometer needle on distant water molecules, for example, makes some difference in the movement of all the molecules they collide with.)

The most common strategy for modifying (PRC-Simplistic) is to hold fixed the presence or absence of other potential background factors. We say that an event C screens E_2 off from E_1 exactly when $P(E_1 \mid E_2 \ \& \ C) = P(E_1 \mid C)$. Unless we are in an unusual situation where $P(E_2 \ \& \ C) = 0$, this equation representing screening-off is the same as $P(E_1 \ \& \ E_2 \mid C) = P(E_1 \mid C) \ P(E_2 \mid C)$, which says intuitively that once the existence of C has been taken for granted, E_1 and E_2 are probabilistically independent. When E_1 and E_2 are probabilistically independent conditional on C, the causal relation between them usually matches the causal chain depicted in either figure 6.1a or figure 6.1b, or it is evidence that C is a common cause of E_1 and E_2, as depicted in figure 6.2.

One can usually infer which of these three models is the best causal interpretation of the probabilistic relations simply by knowing the temporal order in which the events occur.

The standard way to patch the defective principle (PRC-Simplistic) is to equate causation with probability-raising after conditionalizing on appropriate background factors,

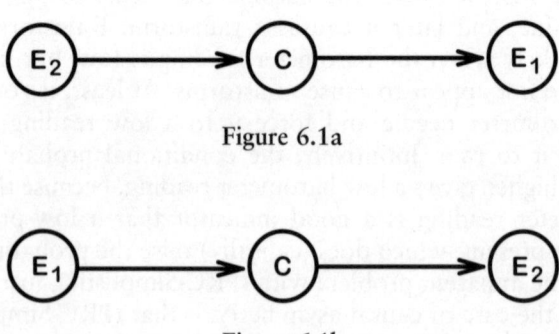

Figure 6.1a

Figure 6.1b

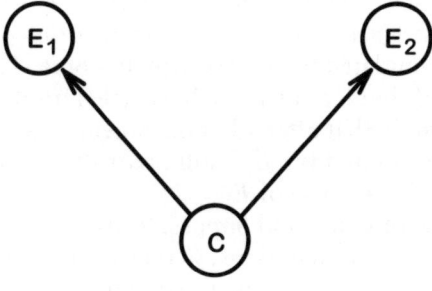

Figure 6.2

including potential common causes. Advocates have formulated this claim in different ways, depending on what background factors they think are appropriate:

(PRC-Reichenbach) C causes E exactly when all of the following conditions hold:
1. C occurs before E
2. $P(C) > 0$
3. $P(E \mid C) > P(E)$
4. There is no event prior to (or simultaneous with) C's occurrence that screens off the correlation between C and E.

(PRC-Good) C causes E to the degree $P(\sim E \mid \sim C \& F)/P(\sim E \mid C \& F)$, measured on a logarithmic scale, where F includes all the background conditions obtaining before C occurs.

(PRC-Suppes) C causes E exactly when all of the following conditions hold:
1. C occurs before E
2. $P(C) > 0$
3. $P(E \mid C) > P(E)$
4. Events earlier than C cannot be distinguished into groups that screen off the correlation between C and E.

(PRC-Cartwright-Eells) C causes E exactly when $P(E \mid C \& B) > P(E \mid B)$ for every state B of E's other causes that are not between C and E.

I cannot stress enough how important it is for you, as someone just starting to learn about theories of causation, not to be intimidated by the mathematics here. The core idea, regardless of how academics have tried to formalize the details, is simply that after all of the potential common causes have been accounted for, if C still raises the probability of E, then C must be a cause of E.

In the case of Good and Suppes, 'cause' is defined without referring to any causal notions, so they are reducing causation to probabilistic relations. In Cartwright's theory, the word 'causes' appears on both sides of the definition, so she is not suggesting that a reduction of causation to probabilistic relations exists.

Simpson's Paradox

The third and final challenge for probability-raising accounts is Simpson's paradox. Edward Simpson (1951) drew attention to a previously known arithmetic truth that can sound counterintuitive when it occurs in the context of conditional probabilities. In a much-cited example, the University of California at Berkeley was sued for having graduate admissions biased against women because women were admitted at significantly lower rates than men. Further statistical analysis (Bickel, Hammel, and O'Connell 1975) showed that, overall, the fraction of women admitted by departments within the graduate school was slightly larger than the fraction of men. Because admissions were made by individual departments and admission to the graduate school was granted to exactly those students accepted by the departments, this data suggested that there was no discernible discrimination against women. Simpson's paradox is the counterintuitive fact that it is possible for every department to admit a larger fraction of women than men but still have the graduate school as a whole admit a larger fraction of men than women. Restricted to any single department, the probability of admission given that the candidate is a woman is greater than the probability of admission given that the candidate is a man. Aggregating the data for the graduate school as a whole, however, results in a so-called Simpson's reversal where the probability of admission given that the candidate is a woman is less than the probability of admission given that the candidate is a man.

The paradox in this example can be explained by recognizing that women tended to apply to the more selective departments.

The problem that Simpson's paradox poses to probability-raising theories of causation is that nothing in their rules (which equate causal relationships with probability-raising relationships) indicates whether the statistical correlations should be separated into department-level data or all grouped together as data for the one graduate school. Given that being female raises the probability of admission in every department, but school-wide lowers the probability of admission, is being female a positive or negative causal factor for admission? It is widely accepted that a causal factor cannot be both probability-raising and probability-lowering for the same effect in the same background circumstances. Probability-raising theories of causation thus appear to need additional theoretical machinery to adjudicate which data indicates the causation: the departmental or graduate school data. In the real world, one can check whether the decisions were made by individual departments by examining the activity of the admissions committees, and in the given example, that seems to indicate that being female did not reduce one's chances of admission to the graduate school. But what kind of information is being used to prefer the departmental statistics to the graduate school statistics? If it were to include information about causal structure, that would rule out a reduction of causal relations to probabilistic relations. In any case, a probability-raising account of causation needs to specify what sort of information is required.

Advantages

Probability-raising accounts of causation help to makes sense of several features of causation:

1. Causation does not require determination. The right kind of reliable probabilistic connection between Cs and Es is arguably enough to vindicate the reasonableness of trying to bring about an E by bringing about a C.

2. Probability-raising accounts establish a sort of difference-making that does not require any appeal to counterfactuals or non-actual possibilities. Because most theories of counterfactuals provide extensive leeway for philosophical mischief, counterfactual dependence is rightly viewed with suspicion. The difference-making defined by probability-raising accounts is no more mysterious than the probabilistic relations they assume. (The probabilistic relations themselves might be unacceptably imprecise.)

3. We often successfully infer causation from statistical frequencies after controlling for other confounding factors. Probability-raising accounts make clear why such data is relevant for establishing causation. Competing accounts, by contrast, need to provide some explanation of how their metaphysical structures support the demonstrated effectiveness of learning about causal generalities from observed statistical frequencies.

Challenges

I have already mentioned the main challenges for any probability-raising account of causation: accommodating causal asymmetry, excluding spurious correlations, and ensuring that no inconsistencies arise from a factor counting as both probability-raising and probability-lowering in the same circumstances. I have not attempted to evaluate whether existing accounts satisfactorily address these problems because space is short.

Instead, for the sake of completeness, I will now describe a somewhat different collection of alleged problems: counter-examples to probability-raising accounts of singular causation. Some advocates of probability-raising accounts of causation, including Suppes, think of probabilistic relations as holding among singular events. Let's consider a version of a probability-raising account of singular causation, simplified to avoid complications introduced to solve the three previously described problems.

> (PRC-Singular) An instance of C is a cause of an instance of E exactly when the C raises the probability of the E in the sense that $P(E \mid C) > P(E)$.

This simple theory of causation, (PRC-Singular), implies that probability-raising is *necessary* for singular causation: Whenever some C was a cause of some E, the C raised the probability of its E. Philosophers have argued that this requirement conflicts with a correct assessment of certain scenarios involving a probability-lowering cause. We have already seen two such cases.

First, the improbable chain of particle decays depicted in figure 3.2, from our discussion of causal process theories, is a counterexample. The decay of particle A into particle B lowered the probability that a D would be created, but a D was created from the B decaying, which makes the decay of particle A into B a cause of D.

Second, another counterexample appeared in our discussion of overdetermination near the end of chapter 4 (Paul 2009). Recall that we imagined two events, c_1 and c_2, with each one determining by itself an effect e. If neither had occurred, e would likely not have occurred. On the one hand, c_1 and c_2 both ought to be counted as causes of e because together they raised the probability of e, e occurred, and they are equal in all respects, including that each was by itself sufficient for e. On the other hand, because c_1 occurred and determined e, c_2 by itself did not raise the probability of e, and because c_2 occurred and determined e, c_1 by itself did not raise the probability of e. Common sense declares both of them to be causes of e, but neither individual event raised e's probability.

It is a fun exercise to construct other counterexamples. Can you imagine a scenario where c does not make any difference to the *probability* of e, but is a cause by virtue of some other interaction between them?

(PRC-Singular) also implies that probability-raising is *sufficient* for singular causation: Whenever c raises the probability of an actually occurring e, the c is a cause of the e.

Philosophers have argued that this sufficient condition conflicts with the two following scenarios that we have already assessed.

Recall the example of preemption from our discussion of difference-making in chapter 4, where the first agent poisons the canteen, and the second agent pokes a hole in the canteen, preempting a poisoning death, but causing a dehydration death. Now, flesh out this example by making clear that the poison is extremely effective, but that the presence of some nearby watering holes gave the traveler a moderate chance of survival even without a full canteen. Thus, by causing the canteen to leak, the second agent was lowering the probability of the traveler's death significantly, yet it was the cause of his death all the same.

As before, one can attempt to rescue the theory of causation by appealing to the transitivity of causation and the chain of intermediate events that led from the canteen leak to the dehydration. Yet, as before, there are other counterexamples that do not depend on any intermediate events. Recall that in the case of overlapping causation in chapter 4, the silver wizard raised the probability of the prince being turned into a frog from 50 percent to 75 percent, and the prince was enfrogged. But we know that the silver wizard was not a cause because his spell targeted the prince and queen together, and the queen remained human.

These counterexamples rebut the proposition that singular causation can be equated with probability-raising, but more sophisticated versions of the hypothesis have been developed, for example in Eells (1991) and Kvart (1986). Also, the problems highlighted by the counterexamples – as we saw when we were considering counterfactual theories of causation in chapter 4 – point to the need to address the contrastive character of many singular causal claims and how broadly to construe the effect. Probability-raising accounts need to be modified to address these issues.

Reichenbach's Common Cause Principle

At this point in the chapter, I have delivered all of the basic information that I intended to convey concerning probability-raising accounts of causation. In the remaining portion of this chapter, I would like to return to one topic – common causes – in a discussion that is a bit more advanced, so if you are feeling at all intimidated with the material discussed so far, feel free to concentrate on reviewing what I have already covered rather than digging into still more controversial territory. The two reasons I want to engage this additional topic are (1) to emphasize the need for greater clarity about what conceptions of events and probability should be used in probability-raising accounts of causation, and (2) to describe a fascinating scientific question that requires philosophical inquiry into causation.

Hans Reichenbach (1956) tried to identify a remarkable causal principle, which he called the principle of the common cause: "If an improbable coincidence has occurred, there must exist a common cause." He illustrates with a scenario in which a pair of lightbulbs go off at the same time. He points out that we would be reasonable to doubt that the two bulbs burned out at the exact same time for independent reasons; instead, we will rightly expect that a single source of electricity has been cut off or that there was a single surge of current that fried both electrical circuits. That is, there is surely a common cause of the two bulbs' going out simultaneously. What's more, it *explains* the coincidence to cite this common cause rather than citing a common effect, like the increased darkness of the room.

But, after providing some additional illustrations, Reichenbach backs off his insistence that there *must* exist a common cause in favor of a claim that there will *likely* be a common cause, and that repeated coincidences of the same type make the presence of a common cause much more likely.

Then, Reichenbach pivots by declaring, "It will be advisable to treat the principle of the common cause as a statistical problem. For this purpose we assume that A and B have been observed to occur frequently; thus it is possible to speak of probabilities $P(A)$, $P(B)$, ..." Unfortunately, Reichenbach does not make clear how the variables representing event types are related to singular events like the two bulbs burning out. He once[3] claimed that the application of probability ascriptions to singular events is "fictive" and that it should be understood in terms of some implicit event type, but what remains unclear is whether there are any constraints on what counts as a permissible event type. I will return to this issue shortly.

Reichenbach's main idea appears to be that, for the most part, whenever two events are probabilistically correlated, there are only three possible explanations. Either e_1 is a cause of e_2, or e_2 is a cause of e_1, or there is a common cause of e_1 and e_2. (Recall figures 6.1 and 6.2.) Reichenbach seems to believe that probabilistic correlations among events can be completely accounted for in terms of causal relationships.

Reichenbach tries to make his 'principle of the common cause' more precise as follows. Let a and b be two singular events (with associated event types A and B) neither of which is a cause of the other, but which are positively correlated. Positive correlation is expressed as

1. $P(A \ \& \ B) > P(A) \ P(B)$.

Reichenbach claimed any such pair of events will have a common cause of type C, obeying the following rules:

2. $P(A \mid C) > P(A \mid {\sim}C)$
3. $P(B \mid C) > P(B \mid {\sim}C)$
4. $P(A \ \& \ B \mid C) = P(A \mid C) \ P(B \mid C)$
5. $P(A \ \& \ B \mid {\sim}C) = P(A \mid {\sim}C) \ P(B \mid {\sim}C)$.

Note that we also need $0 < P(C) < 1$ in order for these equations to be well defined because it does not make sense to divide by zero. Equations 2 and 3 say that C raises the probability of A and B, which is what we should expect when C is a cause of both. Equations 4 and 5 express that A and B no longer remain correlated once we take into account either the existence or absence of C. In the jargon introduced earlier, the presence of C screens off the correlation between A and B, and the absence of C does so as well.

In order to get a more concrete grip on what Reichenbach is communicating with all of these formulas, just consider how they apply to the previously mentioned pair of lightbulbs. Equation 1 claims that the probability of both bulbs going out together is greater than what you should expect if they were independent. That is reasonable because there are causal connections that link them, like the common power source, which could fail. Equation 2 tells us that the probability that the one lightbulb will go out, given that the electricity to the whole building is cut off, is higher than the probability that it will go out given that the electricity supply remains on. The same holds for the other bulb according to equation 3. Equation 4 claims that, given that the electricity remains on, the probability of each bulb going out is independent of the other. Equation 5 states that, given that the electricity shuts off, the probability of each bulb going out is independent of the other.

After reviewing these five principles, your philosophical antennae ought to pick up a troubling signal coming from equation 4. Could there be multiple possible common causes, any one of which renders two effects probabilistically independent of one another? Reichenbach was aware of this and suggested that C can represent disjunctions of common causes. But he did not leave room in his formulation for more complicated combinations of events that could interact with each other to serve together as common causes. Although his formula needs to be tweaked to be completely general, let's not worry about that detail.

These equations do not appear to define what counts as a common cause, and Reichenbach did not provide a formal definition of 'common cause'. (As applied to singular actual events, a common cause c of e_1 and e_2 is presumably an event that was a cause of e_1 and a cause of e_2. The problem is that Reichenbach does not relate this conception to his formulas, and it is not clear how to fix the missing component of the theory.) An event can intuitively be a common cause of e_1 and e_2 without satisfying all these equations, and an event can satisfy all these equations without being a common cause of e_1 and e_2. As an exercise, you can prove that in figure 6.3, d is intuitively a common cause of a and b, but it does not screen them off because of c. Also, e is intuitively not a common cause of a and b, but all of Reichenbach's equations can easily be made true (with e playing the role of C).[4]

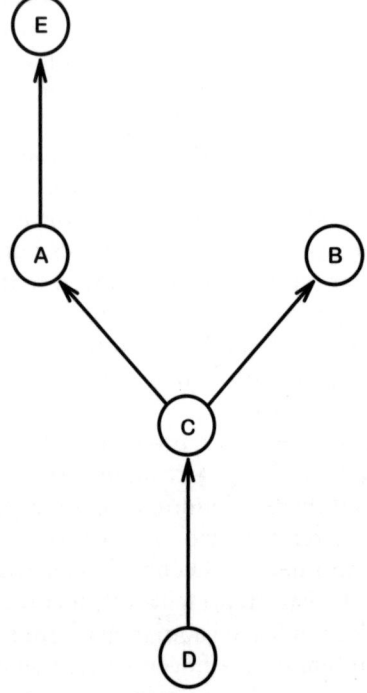

Figure 6.3

The Unclear Relationship between Probability and Singular Events

It is a smart move for us now to return to an observation I made earlier, when Reichenbach muddied the conceptual waters somewhat by switching the definition of a common cause from holding among event tokens to holding among event types.

He assigns probabilities to singular events on the basis of some statistical regularities, but he never adequately defines the relationship between a singular event and its event types. For example, we know that a single event can be a token of many types, which raises the question of which types should be used (or be allowed) to assign a singular event a determinate probabilistic value. This has led to significant confusion about what kinds of phenomena could count as violations of the principle of the common cause.

Let us now consider some proposed counterexamples to Reichenbach's principle in an effort to understand what relations exist between singular events and the probabilities that are derived from statistics among events of a certain type.

For our first example, consider Elliott Sober's (2001) observation that the price of bread in London correlates with the sea level in Venice. Both have been continually rising over the past century or so, but presumably for unrelated reasons. Chris Hitchcock (2012) has argued that Reichenbach has in mind a more limited conception of probabilistic correlation. Hitchcock says,

> Choose some particular time t, and let A_t and B_t be events involving the sea level in Venice and the price of bread in London at t (respectively). Now it's not clear that we can make any sense of a probability assignment in which $P(A_t$ & $B_t) > P(A_t)P(B_t)$. In particular, sampling sea levels and bread prices at times *other than t* is not an appropriate method for estimating these probabilities, since we are not sampling from a stationary distribution. (By analogy, we would not say that I had a probability of 2/3 of being over six feet tall on my third birthday, just because I have been over six feet tall on roughly two-thirds of the birthdays I have ever had.)

Hitchcock's idea here – which is correct – is that some collections of events of the same type are not suitable for the attribution of probability. The problem, though, is that neither Reichenbach nor other advocates of probability-raising accounts of causation have provided clear enough rules for which data samples are admissible.

For a second example, consider another situation recounted by Hitchcock where a mixture of giraffes and rhinos exists, with the giraffes being taller and having better eyesight. Height and good vision are correlated in this population even when the rhino and giraffe traits have no causal relationship. The correlation does disappear if we consider them as two separate populations (or take into account their genes), but species membership does not seem to count as an event that can serve as a common cause.

To summarize, a big problem with Reichenbach's principle of the common cause is that the details have not yet been specified precisely enough in order to understand how talk of probability applies to events. If this were just a problem with Reichenbach or common cause principles in general, it might be of limited interest, but the same charge can be leveled to some degree against all probability-raising accounts of causation.

Conjunctive Forks

Besides helping to cast light on the problem of how to apply probabilities sensibly to particular happenings, Reichenbach's (1956) principle of the common cause also provides a glimpse into the fascinating topic of how causation relates to time. In particular, Reichenbach intended his common cause principle to help "define" the direction of time.

Reichenbach's basic idea was that nature exhibits a pattern in which singular events of type C that satisfy the common cause principle all happen to be situated on the same temporal side of a corresponding A and B (as are other instances of C that serve as common causes of corresponding As and Bs).

Let's look at this in more detail. When two correlated events of types A and B have an event of type C that satisfies (all the equations in) the principle of the common cause, we say there is a **conjunctive fork**. If, in addition, there is an event of type D that occurs on the opposite temporal side of A and B from C, and the combination of A, B, and D satisfies (all the equations in) the principle of the common cause, we say that the ABC conjunctive fork is closed by D (figure 6.4).

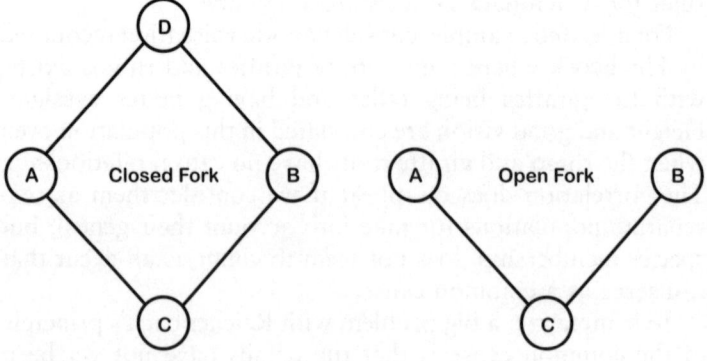

Figure 6.4

The *ABD* fork is also closed by *C*. If there is no such event *D*, the conjunctive fork *ABC* is said to be open. Reichenbach hypothesizes that in fact all (or perhaps almost all) existing forks are open toward the same temporal direction. He then proposes that we define 'future' to be the direction of time in which forks are open, and 'past' to be the other direction.

In retrospect, I think that Reichenbach's work here should be understood as an attempt to provide an identification of that feature of the world that best explains why the two directions of time differ from each other qualitatively. What's more, he does not choose the easy route as Hume does by simply positing a fundamental future direction; Reichenbach appears to think the direction of time is non-fundamental. That said, his work on the direction of time is unfortunately imprecise. In particular, he does not clarify which aspects of time he is attempting to explain and which are left unexplained. He also does not articulate what problem or problems his theory is intended to address. For example, if we are interested in explaining why we cannot influence the past, it is not clear how the fork asymmetry would fit in. Why does causation toward the past require conjunctive forks open to the past?

Furthermore, Reichenbach's failure to make clear the relation between singular and general causation raises trouble again because he was operating on the background assumption that the fundamental laws were (or at least could be) deterministic toward both the future and past. As Frank Arntzenius (1990) pointed out, for any conjunctive fork *ABC*, we can apply the fundamental laws to a state instantiating the event type *C* and it will determine a state instantiating some event type *D* on the opposite temporal side of *A* and *B* that satisfies the common cause principle and thus forms a conjunctive fork *ABD*. Therefore, when the laws are deterministic, Reichenbach's theory appears to imply that all conjunctive forks are closed, in which case they cannot define which direction is the future. There is perhaps a way to salvage Reichenbach's theory by arguing that common causes in the past tend to be characterizable *simply*, whereas the kinds of common effects generated by Arntzenius's procedure are almost certainly extremely complex and convoluted types. Such a strategy, though, is probably going to struggle to make sense of a principled difference between simple and complex event types because that seems to be a matter of degree and because it might depend too much on (arguably idiosyncratic) human standards for identifying simplicity.

In any case, without settling the question of how best to understand the fork asymmetry, we should commend Reichenbach for his effort to provide at least a hint of a scientific explanation of why the past appears to be so different from the future. It is much more difficult to construct a scientific model that casts light on a long-standing philosophical puzzle like the direction of time than to refute the latest theory of singular causation with an intuitively gripping counterexample.

Questions

Q: You said there are hardly any cases where c causes e and e causes c, but what about if you have two books leaning against one another? Each one is causing the other to remain upright.

A: Your example is intuitively striking, but I think it obscures the underlying reality that microscopically there is a slight delay so that each book at time t causes the other book just afterward at time $t + \varepsilon$ to remain standing, and then this future-directed causation keeps recurring from each book to the other. So it is *a kind* of symmetric causation, I suppose, at a folksy level of description, but it is fundamentally asymmetric according to our current understanding of the forces that keep the books apart.

Q: What is the difference between probability and chance?

A: First, chance is a subspecies of probability in the sense that a chance is a quantity that obeys the axioms of probability. Precisely how chances differ from other kinds of probability is difficult to answer because so many of the interpretations of probability either do not make sense or have not been adequately characterized. But caveats aside, I think it is handy to think of a chance in terms of a probabilistic extension of determination. Remember that determination accounts of causation are defective because they can only accommodate cases where the cause guarantees the occurrence of the effect. The main advantage of probability-raising theories of causation is that they appear to apply directly to probabilistic causation and to determination as a special case.

Suppose we try to fix this deficiency of determination accounts of causation by allowing causes to *determine a probability* for the occurrence of certain kinds of effects rather than determining the effects themselves. The basic idea here would be to start with the complete state of the universe c at some chosen time, with a law dictating a specific probability that a certain kind of event E will be instantiated at a prescribed later time. Then, imagine Mother Nature randomly selecting from all the allowed possibilities exactly one possibility to actualize for the near-term future. Her choice should be weighted according to the lawful probabilities, but she should not use any other principle. For example, if the state of the universe includes a person just starting to flip a coin and determines that the probability of its landing heads is one-half, then Mother Nature should somehow make an equally weighted random selection between heads and tails, completely ignoring that the six previous coin flips were all tails. Chance, as I understand it, is the kind of probability used in this model of how the universe evolves.

To relate this all back to causation, chance can be seen as a form of probability that a productive conception of causation could incorporate in order to help explain the statistical frequencies we observe. Chanciness is thus part of a theory competing against the probability-raising accounts we have discussed in this chapter.

Further Reading

The next step to take in learning about probabilistic theories of causation is to examine Williamson's (2009) entry in the *Oxford Handbook of Causation* and then Chris Hitchcock's (2012) entry "Probabilistic Causation" in the *Stanford Encyclopedia of Philosophy*. Good information on Reichenbach and his principle of the common cause can also be found in the *Stanford Encyclopedia of Philosophy*.

7
Manipulation and Intervention

One of the four distinctions I introduced in chapter 1 to help categorize various approaches to causation was the difference between pattern-based and influence-based aspects of causation. Again, recall Dummett's (1964) "intelligent tree," which finds it convenient to have some sort of conception of causation but has no need to think of causation in terms of influence, agency, manipulation, or intervention.

In this chapter, we are going to examine a tradition that has focused on the influence-based aspects. The central idea in this current of thought is that causal relations are potential routes by which the world can be manipulated or controlled. First, we will look at some early views that proposed defining causation partially in terms of agency. We will then trace this line of thought to the idea that we need causal concepts because we need to draw a distinction between effective and ineffective strategies for manipulating the world. This transition de-emphasizes the role of agency in causation to accommodate causation in the inanimate world more naturally.

Finally, we will arrive at the most prominent contemporary approach in the manipulationist tradition, the interventionist approach to causation based on causal modeling, which shifts the attention from agency to the less anthropocentric notion of intervention.

Manipulationist Theories

The motivating thesis behind manipulationist theories of causation is that causes are handles for bringing about or preventing their corresponding effects. The novelty in the manipulationist tradition is that they treat agency as *essential* to causation in the sense that what makes a relation fully causal has something to do with the ability of agents to manipulate aspects of the world.

Von Wright's Formulation

An early proponent, Georg Henrik von Wright (1971a, 1971b, 1974), formulated this idea in terms of what he called a manipulative or experimentalist idea of causation. According to von Wright (1971b, p. 74), "*that p* is the cause of *q . . . means* that I could bring about *q*, if I could do (so that) *p*."

One criticism of his suggestion that causes should be defined in terms of what an agent could do is that most causal relations have little or nothing to do with agency. Here is how von Wright (1971a, p. 306) responds:

> By no means have I wanted to maintain that the operation of a cause always results from action. Causation, needless to say, operates throughout nature independently of agency, also in regions of the world forever inaccessible to human interference. But the test procedures characteristic of causal laws, including those whose operation is far removed from us in space or time, belong to the scientists' laboratories – and they belong there *essentially*, because of their conceptual connection with the mode of action we call experiment.

In other places, von Wright emphasizes that the "dependence of causation upon action is *conceptual*," and that we need to have some agential conception of manipulation or interfering with the usual procession of events in order to distinguish between causal laws and accidental regularities.

So how are causal claims about planets and stars essentially based on the concept of a deliberate action?

> When a regularity is recorded between phenomena which are not subject to direct interference by manipulation – for example because they take place in remote parts of the universe – we are, I think, on the whole hesitant to speak of them as "causally related" or of the regularity as a "causal law." The regularity is rather what Mill (1843) called an "empirical law". . . . Our knowledge of causes and effects in remote regions in space, or, as in geological or paleontological research, in time, is based on and "mediated" by our knowledge of natural laws for which we have sufficient experimental evidence from our laboratories. (von Wright 1974, pp. 308–9)

So von Wright's defense is to clarify that what he means by a 'manipulative' idea of causation is that the scientific conception of causation, embodied in laboratory practice, incorporates the concept of manipulation but also applies in cases where there is no manipulation.

The main advantage von Wright cites for his conception of causation is that it can explain the asymmetry of causation. In many cases, an event c determines an event e and vice versa, yet c is a cause of e with e not being a cause of c. He points out that because rains cause flooding, we can often correctly infer from the absence of flooding to the lack of (heavy) rain. Yet, because we cannot "imagine" (1974, p. 307) ways of controlling rain by controlling floods, and we can imagine controlling floods by controlling rainfall, we can isolate a feature of the world that distinguishes cause from effect. The asymmetry of causation consists in the general truth that an event can be manipulated through its causes but never through its effects.

Menzies and Price's Formulation

The (1993) article "Causation as a Secondary Quality" by Peter Menzies and Huw Price advanced the manipulationist tradition by articulating what they call an agency theory of causation. The principle governing agency theories of causation is the following rule:

> An event c is a cause of a distinct event e just in case bringing about the occurrence of c would be an effective means by which a free agent could bring about the occurrence of e.

The main interpretive issue that needs to be addressed is how to construe 'free agent', and then there are some more pointed criticisms, especially how to construe 'bringing about' without circularly defining it in terms of causation.

Menzies and Price's agency theory does not define 'free agent' but it does connect the pre-theoretical conception of agency most people have with the concept of causation. Specifically, it defines an **agent probability**, $p_C(E)$, to be "the probability that should enter into the calculations of a rational agent whose abilities consist in the capacity to realize or to prevent [C], and whose goals turn entirely on [E]" (1993, p. 190). It then measures the degree to which C is an effective means for bringing about E as $p_C(E) - p_{-C}(E)$. The overall idea is to measure the degree of causation from C to E by evaluating the difference in the probability E would have if an agent simply made C come about vs. what it would be if an agent made C not occur. So the agency theory here is proposing to understand causation as a form of probability-raising, but the introduction of the idea that the agent is somehow intervening in the world means that Menzies and Price's account does not face the same challenges as the probability-raising accounts we encountered in chapter 6.

Challenges

One question about Menzies and Price's agency theory is, "How does it explain causal relations among events that have nothing to do with agency?" Their answer is that causation can reasonably be attributed in a scenario when its intrinsic features are similar enough to a scenario where an agent does freely bring about the cause in order to bring about an effect. A real earthquake may be said to have been caused by friction between continental plates, they suggest, because it shares enough intrinsic features with a seismologist's artificial simulation of the earthquake.

If you think that answer makes too much of the role of agency, you are not alone. How can agency be essential to causation when, if you removed all human beings, there would still be stars causing planets to move in ellipses, there would still be winds causing erosion, and so on? The answer from Menzies and Price's perspective is that causation in this respect is no different from colors. What makes blue objects blue is not a common chemical or physical structure; blue objects are categorized together because of how they affect humans and other creatures with color vision. Tracing the analogy further, we can agree that blue objects would still be blue if no one saw them, but that would not take away the fact that the category of 'blue' is carved out the way it is because of how color perceivers reliably respond to various patterns of light.

Huw Price (forthcoming) has more recently proposed an answer that goes one step further by disavowing that the agency theory concerns the metaphysics of causation. Instead, he suggests it should be understood as explaining why creatures like us would come to speak and think in causal terms. The idea here is that the agency theory of causation is not trying to tell us what causation ultimately is, but instead why we conceive of causation the way we do. This answer serves to limit the ambitions of the agency theory, but as a result, it is unclear whom the argument is trying to convince. Who has ever denied that one justification for conceiving of the world's operation in causal terms is that manipulating causes is a good way to achieve desired effects?

Another question about the agency theory is how to understand what it could mean for an agent to bring about an effect without defining "bringing about" in terms of causation. Menzies and Price do not provide any hint as to how we should understand "bringing about" formally, but instead just attempt to rebut the charge of circularity by suggesting that as children, we acquaint ourselves instinctively with the agential way of bringing about effects. Then, when we theorize about causation as adults, we can rely on this pre-conceived notion of bringing about an effect to define a more technical concept of causation.

Effective Strategies

As Michael Dummett (1964) observed, our concept of causation incorporates an agent-centric aspect. We often think of causes as being means by which a chosen type of effect can be brought about. And we show a preference for citing the actions of agents as causes rather than other kinds of causes, like background enabling conditions and events in the expected course of nature.

Another gloss on this idea is to recognize that there is a demonstrable difference between effective and ineffective strategies for affecting the world, and causation seems to be an obvious candidate to help explain why some strategies are more effective than others. The label 'effective strategies' appears first in a (1979) article by Nancy Cartwright, who recounted the following anecdote concerning a letter she received from TIAA-CREF, a company which provides insurance for college teachers. The letter begins:

> It simply wouldn't be true to say,
>
> > "Nancy L. D. Cartwright . . . if you own a TIAA life insurance policy you'll live longer."
>
> But it is a fact, nonetheless, that persons insured by TIAA do enjoy longer lifetimes, on the average, than persons insured by commercial insurance companies that serve the general public.

It is uncontroversial that buying a TIAA life insurance policy is not an effective strategy for living longer. What Cartwright argues is that we need distinctively *causal* laws in order to explain why some strategies are more effective than others. We cannot get by with "laws of association," which indicate statistical relationships or other patterns in the historical layout of the universe. Even if there are comprehensive laws of physics that indicate how the future and past must be, given how things are presently arranged, we need something extra to explain why some strategies are effective and others are not. We need laws that invoke causality.

Cartwright, as we discussed in chapter 6, advocated a probability-raising account of causation and did not attempt to define causation in terms of agency. Instead, the task of explaining the agent-centric distinction between effective and ineffective strategies is being advanced as a condition of adequacy for theories of causation. Any good account of causation, the thought goes, needs to make sense of the range of cases where two kinds of events appear regularly together or are statistically correlated, but where neither is a good means for bringing about the other. As an independent research project, you can evaluate for yourself whether Cartwright explains why some strategies for manipulating the world are more effective than others.

Interventionist Accounts

Since the beginning of this century, much of the overall research on causation has attended to the literature on causal modeling, building on the work of Judea Pearl (2000), Peter Spirtes, Clark Glymour, and Richard Scheines (2000), Jim Woodward (2003), and others.[1] One central purpose of this literature is to provide a generic structure for understanding (mostly special science) causation, including singular and general causation.

The accounts of causation in this literature are labeled 'interventionist' because the feature that most distinguishes them from probabilistic accounts of causation is the introduction of an additional conceptual device – the intervention – to represent an external manipulation of a causal system.

The interventionist framework accepts that causal relations can be found using current scientific practices such as double-blind placebo-controlled medical trials. Proving the existence of causal relationships, in this approach, does not require ascertaining whether there is a law covering the tested relations or understanding how to model the logic of counterfactuals or settling philosophical questions about what causation ultimately amounts to. Thus, interventionist theories are non-metaphysical in the sense that they are insulated from whether causation reduces to fundamental laws and the historical arrangement of matter in the universe. Instead, they attempt to draw a wealth of connections among the scientific practice of discovering and testing causal claims, supplying causal and mechanistic explanations, and describing causal reasoning.

Causal Modeling

Causal models are defined formally as a set of variables (and the range of their possible values) together with structural equations that specify the direct causal relationships among them. These equations imply indirect causal relationships. Causal models are often depicted using directed graphs, where each node corresponds to a single variable, and each arrow corresponds to a direct causal relationship expressed by a structural equation. The structural equations define the values of some variables in terms of others. Any variable whose value is assigned by a structural equation is an **endogenous** variable, which means it represents part of the internal causal structure captured by the model. Any variable whose value is not assigned by a structural equation is an **exogenous** variable, which means it represents a background condition and is incorporated into the model only as an externally specified input value. Most background conditions do not appear as variables but are just built into the model. A causal model of how buffalo roam will not include a variable for the earth's gravitational pull but will just assume the constant gravity as a presupposition for the adequacy of the equations defining the speed and stamina of the herd.

For the sake of illustration, assume we are investigating the delicacy of the ecosystem in a coral reef and construct a model with the following variables. Let's say we are interested in whether implementing "reforestation" techniques is effective in fostering biodiversity in a coral reef. The following causal model might be considered a first step in the research program.

R the rate of chemical run-off into the ocean.
V the amount of wild vegetation on the coast.
P the population of people inhabiting surrounding areas.
A the fraction of land used for agriculture.
B the biodiversity of the reef.

Suppose that the relations among the variables are captured by the following structural equations.

$$B = f_1(P, R)$$
$$R = f_2(P, A, V)$$
$$V = f_3(A)$$
$$P = f_4(A)$$

A couple of points to note:

- The equations define the value of the variable on the left in terms of the value of the variable on the right, quantifying the influence from the variables on the right to the variable on the left. The equations mathematically imply that $P = f_4(f_3^{-1}(V))$ when f_3^{-1} is well-defined, but that should not be interpreted as V influencing P.
- Each variable appears on the left at most once. Variables that appear on the left are said to be *endogenous*. Variables that do not appear on the left are *exogenous*; any values they have must be "plugged in" because they cannot be derived from other quantities in the model.
- The relations among the variables can be depicted in a directed graph by (1) drawing exactly one node for each variable, and (2) inserting an arrow from one node to another where the 'to' node corresponds to a variable on the left side of a structural equation and the 'from' node corresponds to a variable on the right side of that same equation. (It will normally turn out that all the nodes are linked together because if a single node is unlinked, that would mean its variable does not affect anything, and if two or more groups of nodes are unlinked the model can be redescribed as separate models.) Figure 7.1 is an example of a graph derived from our structural equations.

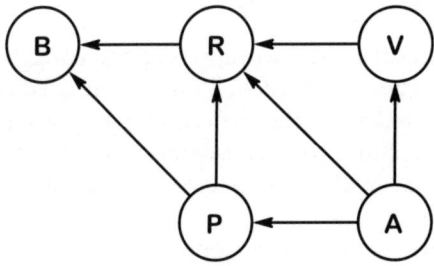

Figure 7.1

We say that V has a **direct effect** on R because there is an arrow that goes directly from V to R. We say that V has an **indirect effect** on B because there is a path following multiple arrows that goes from V to B.

What matters in the causal graph are which values are connected to which other values, not where the nodes appear in the drawing. Because the structural equations are express-ing directed relationships among quantities in nature, we can interpret the arrow from P to B as signifying that the value of P influences the value of B, but not that the value of B influences the value of P. Typically, P will not by itself deter-mine the value of B; the specific value of R will be needed as well.

We can also see from the graph which variables are endog-enous; they label nodes with arrows going *to* them. An exog-enous variable always labels a node with all arrows going *away from* it.

How do the structural equations and graph relate to causa-tion? To begin, we can usually restrict consideration to the special case of acyclic graphs, where there are no paths of arrows that return to a previously visited node. In figure 7.1, we see that every path eventually leads to B and stops, so it is an acyclic graph. (The two paths from A that fork to P and R and then recombine at B do not constitute a causal loop.) For the special case of acyclic graphs, a specification of the values of the exogenous variables is enough to determine the value for all the variables. In this case, a specification of A is enough to determine V, P, R, and B. So one activity involving the graph and structural equations is to go out to a bunch of reefs, measure all these variables, and check how accurate the structural equations are.

For the causal model to represent the causal structure of reefs, the measurements of V, P, R, and B need to match the values calculated from the structural equations and the measurement of A. But a good causal model does more. It informs us about what will happen if we manipulate one of the variables.

Imagine the government stepping in and implementing a program that increases the vegetation on the coast without influencing the density of agriculture. In that case, we can use the structural equations to predict P, R, and B, given the measured value of A and the value of V set by the government's activity. We ignore the $V = f_3(A)$ equation because it states the relationship between V and A when the vegetation is left to expand or recede as nature dictates.

By measuring P, R, and B, we get an additional test of whether the structural equations are correct. Without government intervention, the value of R is defined by the model in terms of A, V, and P, but it ultimately depends only on the one independent variable A. With government intervention, the value of R is determined by two independent variables, V and A. This allows us to check the accuracy of the model over a wider range of conditions.

In brief, a causal model provides predictions about the default operation of the target system as well as predictions about what will happen if we intervene to set the endogenous variables to values that would otherwise have been set by a structural equation.

Intervention can be defined in terms of the causal relations established by a model's structural equations. According to the Woodward (2003) version, I counts as an intervention exactly when it satisfies all of the following conditions:

1. I must be the only cause of V.
2. I must not cause B via a route that does not go through V.
3. I should not itself be caused by any cause that affects B via a route that does not go through V.
4. I must be probabilistically independent of any cause of B that does not lie on a causal route connecting V to B.

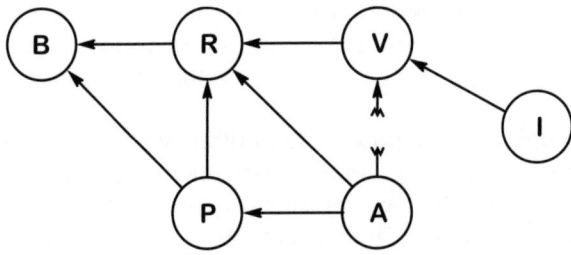

Figure 7.2

An intervention I on the variable V can be depicted by altering figure 7.1 as shown in figure 7.2.

Our causal model satisfies condition 1 because the only arrow going to V is I. It satisfies condition 2 because every path from I to B – and in this case there is only one – goes through V. It satisfies condition 3 because there are no nodes that influence I. The purpose of condition 4 is to rule out cases where some non-causal correlation exists between the value of I and the values of A or P. The graph and structural equations do not guarantee that actual interventions will satisfy condition 4, but it is a condition that is easily satisfied in many common situations.

The individual arrows represent a form of influence, but it is somewhat misleading to say the arrow from V to R designates that coastal vegetation causes the farm's chemical run-off. In our example, higher values of V make for lower values of R because increased vegetation on the coast inhibits the chemical run-off. A better description is that V is **causally relevant** to R. Still, the model can establish when a relation of probability-raising holds between variables.

Questions

That's a lot of information. Why don't we pause here for a couple of questions.

Q: Is interventionism saying that causation is probability-raising but we just use the causal model to figure out when probabilities are raised rather than conditionalizing?

A: I think that is a good way to think about it. Technically, interventionism does not have to involve probability, and when it does, it is neutral between probability-raising and probability-lowering, but insofar as we want to connect it to our ordinary language, I think it is a reasonable gloss on interventionism to say that when V raises the probability of B or raises the value of B, that justifies the conclusion that adding vegetation to the coast causes biodiversity to increase.

The difference between interventionist and standard probability-raising accounts of causation is best captured in the difference between seeing and doing. Judea Pearl (2000) distinguished two functions in terms of the variables X and Y: See and Do. $See(X = x_1, Y)$ takes as input all of the observed data when there are no interventions occurring, discards every observation except those where the variable X takes the value x_1, and then outputs the distribution of Y's values. The difference in Y's distribution given by $See(X = x_1, Y)$ and $See(X = x_2, Y)$ measures the correlation between X's being x_1 and X's being x_2. That encompasses the probability-raising approach where we identify the causal difference-making of X's being x_1 rather than x_2 with $P(Y = y \mid X = x_1) - P(Y = y \mid X = x_2)$. With probability-raising accounts and with the See function, we conditionalize on the variable X and then simply observe the results, leaving all endogenous processes of the system to function as usual.

The other relationship Pearl distinguishes is represented by the Do function, which implements an intervention. $Do(X = x_1, Y)$ takes all the observed data when we intervene to set the value of the variable X at x_1, and then outputs the distribution of Y's values. The difference in Y's distribution given by $Do(X = x_1, Y)$ and $Do(X = x_2, Y)$ measures the causal impact on Y of X's being x_1 rather than x_2. This sort of relation is not captured by standard probability-raising accounts of causation.

In this sense, the causal modeling approach is a more general framework for evaluating causation. Intervening is often more informative than observing because it allows for systematic observation of the effects of a single component in the system. Without intervention, one can only observe the net effects of the totality of exogenous variables on the totality of endogenous variables.

Q: How does interventionism fit into those categories we are supposed to think about?

A: I see interventionism as primarily concerned with general causation, although you can use it to formulate claims about singular causation. It is definitely influence-based. I think it should be considered a difference-making account, but there might be a subtlety there. On the one hand, interventionism is often characterized as a counterfactual approach to causation because the structural equations tell us what would happen if we were to intervene on V by increasing the amount of vegetation by 5 percent. On other hand, you could think of the structural equations as defining how the values of some variables *produce* the values of the variables that lie causally downstream. Because the interventionist measure of difference-making is defined in terms of the counterfactual dependence defined by this sort of production, you might say it is both a productive and a difference-making account.

Path-Specific Causation

We can define some other causal concepts in terms of causal models. Specifically, we can draw a distinction between a total effect of A on B and a contributing effect of A on B. We say that A is a **total cause** of B (and that A has a total effect on B) whenever some interventions on A result in a change in differences to the value of B. We say that A is a **contributing cause** of B (and that A has a contributing effect on B) whenever there is a causal path from A to B and interventions on A result in a change in differences to the value of B while holding fixed the values of any other variables that lie on a path from A to B.

This concept of a contributing causal relation captures the sense in which there can be causation specific to one path even if there is no net influence. We can illustrate path-specific causation using Hesslow's (1981) classic thrombosis example. Taking a birth control pill regularly is a promoter of thrombosis by virtue of its direct role as a chemical in the body. But the birth control pill is also an inhibitor of pregnancy, which itself raises the likelihood of thrombosis. So there are two causal routes by which thrombosis is probabilistically influenced.

We can clarify this scenario using the resources provided by the structural equations. Taking birth control pills is a contributing cause of thrombosis because if we hold fixed the lack of pregnancy, taking birth control pills raises the probability of thrombosis. But taking birth control pills does not have a total effect on thrombosis if they prevent pregnancy and thereby reduce the overall risk back to what it would be without taking the pills.

Singular Causation

The assumed goal of a theory of singular causation is to identify, for any given causal scenario and any choice of effect in that scenario, the causes of that particular effect. As usual, the simple interventionist accounts have been found to mismatch experts' judgments and have been redesigned in a more complicated fashion in an attempt to address the alleged counterexamples without introducing any further undesired mismatches.

Let's briefly cover the Halpern and Pearl (2001, 2005) model of singular causation by examining a simplified version of it in order to avoid getting bogged down in technicalities. To keep matters even simpler, we can use deterministic structural equations that govern binary variables, variables that can only take the value TRUE or FALSE.

The three binary variables in Halpern's causal model are L, C, and F, representing three events: whether lightning

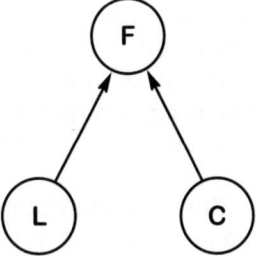

Figure 7.3

strikes a forest, whether the one camper in the area neglects his campfire, and whether a wildfire rages through the forest. The value TRUE represents that the event occurs, and FALSE that the event does not occur. The only structural equation in the model is $F = L$ or C, representing that a forest fire will definitely occur if lightning strikes or if the camper neglects his campfire (or both), and that if neither occurs, there will definitely be no forest fire (figure 7.3).

The theory claims that L is a cause of F exactly when all three of the following conditions hold:

1. L and F occur.
2. Holding fixed everything besides the variables on the path from L to F, an intervention to make L not occur makes F not occur.
3. There is no submodel that satisfies conditions 1 and 2.

Suppose that in the actual world, lightning strikes, the camper does not neglect his campfire, and then a fire ensues. In that case, we can evaluate the counterfactual possibility where the lightning did not strike by using the structural equation to infer that there would have been no forest fire. In this case, common sense dictates that the lightning was a cause of the fire, and Halpern and Pearl's model generates this result.

However, let us now suppose that in the actual world, lightning strikes, and the camper neglects his campfire, and a fire ensues. In that case, we can evaluate the counterfactual possibility that the lightning did not strike by using the structural equation to infer that there still would have been a forest fire (because of the neglected campfire). The natural judgment to make about this scenario is that the lightning was a cause of the fire in addition to the campfire. But Halpern and Pearl's model generates the incorrect result that the lightning was not a cause (because there would have been a fire regardless).

To accommodate this counterexample, Halpern (2008) invokes the idea of an extended causal model, which is a list of models that set various values of the variables not on the main causal path to default values instead of their actual values. The elements in the list are ranked in terms of how much each deviates from normality. The modified theory states that L is a cause of F exactly when the three specified conditions hold either for the actual world or for a world that is relatively unexceptional.

Essentially, Halpern is suggesting that the reason why it is correct to say that the lightning is a cause of the fire (even though it made no difference to whether there was a fire) is that we have a reasonable conception of the typical or normal background conditions. Because it is relatively rare for fires to start, we can ignore the neglected campfire when evaluating whether the fire counterfactually depended on the lightning. And if we pretend that the neglected campfire was not present, as we just saw, the lightning does make a difference as to whether there is a fire.

Advantages

This chapter has discussed manipulationist, interventionist, and causal modeling approaches, and these are neither exactly the same nor clear alternatives. One might say they are variations on a central theme: that one of the main reasons we care about causation is that causes are often means by which we can bring about effects or make them more likely.

1. One of the main selling points for the causal modeling approach in particular is the explicit connection with scientific work on general causation. If scientists are making

demonstrable progress identifying causal regularities and causal models are the tools that help them achieve success, then any reasonable theory of causation should help to make sense of this success. Defining causation in terms of the model is a good way to make the relationship clear.

2.   Another benefit of the causal modeling approach is its close connection with causal explanation. When explaining why certain effects are reliably correlated with certain manipulable inputs, we are often interested in finding the invariant structures that make the obtained effects not surprising, and this is what the structural equations provide. Structural equations also help to predict the effects of interventions, which can often be experimentally tested, thereby earning some scientific credibility that competing theories lack. Counterfactual theories in particular posit untestable rules for how to evaluate what would happen in non-actual scenarios.

3.   At various points in our discussion, we have touched on the distinction between productive and difference-making conceptions of causation. The causal modeling literature shows how these can fit together. The structural equations provide the rules for how nature (insofar as the model represents it) evolves toward the future. Interventions provide a way of quantifying difference-making relations.

Challenges

1.   Nothing rules out the possibility of multiple causal models being adequate for the same causal system. Thus, causal relations hold only relative to a model. This raises the question of whether the model relativity of the causal model approach provides so few constraints that someone can defend false causal claims by simply contriving an ad hoc causal model.

2.   One criticism of the accounts of singular causation that have been developed using causal models is that they require us to supplement the structural equations with a theory of how to set default values for the variables. Hall (2007) provides examples where our identification of the causes in two scenarios differs even though they satisfy the

same causal model. The worry raised is that adding a theory of the default values will never suffice to recover common sense intuitions about test cases.

3. One observation about the entire manipulationist and interventionist approach is that it is non-reductive in the sense that it does not attempt to define causation in terms of non-causal concepts. This is not a defect per se, but we should not expect the approach to provide an explanation of why causal modeling is effective in a wide range of scientific disciplines, or an explanation of why causation is directed toward the future, or an explanation of the circumstances in which causal modeling is ineffective.

Further Reading

Probably the best articles to read for additional depth are the two surveys by Hitchcock (2009b) and Woodward in the (2009) *Oxford Handbook of Causation*. For more detail, consult the standard philosophical reference for interventionist and causal modeling, Woodward's (2003) *Making Things Happen*. Other classics are Judea Pearl's (2000) *Causality* and the Spirtes, Glymour, and Scheines (2000) *Causation, Prediction, and Search*.

8
Mental Causation

We have completed our survey of the broad conceptual land-scape of causation. Because it is easy to get lost in all the detail and controversy, it will be useful for us in this final chapter to review how different theories of causation apply to a single example. I have chosen to focus on the topic of mental causation because it is widely discussed, it is representative of other varieties of causation, and the sorts of confusion that exist in the literature on mental causation provide an excellent opportunity for us to exercise our philosophical abilities by invoking the theories we have previously explored.

Let's start things off with a broad observation. Most of what we are concerned about in life is mental. Our hopes, our emotions, our perceptions, our commitments are all mental. Yet we inhabit a world that is mostly non-mental: a universe with galaxies, rock, water, bacteria, and so on. The age-old puzzle known as the mind–body problem is the question "How do the mental and non-mental fit together?"

Seemingly, *causation* is one way the mental and non-mental are bound together. The sun can cause a sensation of warmth. A decision to stroll through the woods causes a chain of events that eventuate in footprints being created. By attending to such cases, we might be able to use what we have learned about causation to make progress on the mind–body problem.

It is always a good strategy, when dealing with any complex problem, to start with some simplifications. Let's do that by attending initially to just two schematic solutions to the question of how mental and non-mental entities can interact.

Materialism can be understood as the claim that everything in fundamental reality is material. It can be made more even specific as a form of physicalism, which claims that fundamental reality only includes the kinds of entities postulated by physicists: space-time, fields, particles, masses, charges, and so on. All forms of mental causation – mental to non-mental, non-mental to mental, and mental to mental – are merely special cases of what is ultimately just physical to physical causation. (Don't forget that we encountered materialism back in chapter 2.)

Dualism can be understood as the claim that everything in the actual world is fundamentally either physical or spiritual (in the sense of a disembodied soul or a ghostly presence). Mental to non-mental causation is ultimately spiritual to physical causation. Non-mental to mental causation is ultimately physical to spiritual causation. Mental to mental causation is ultimately spiritual to spiritual causation. And non-mental to non-mental causation is ultimately physical to physical causation.

After evaluating the relative merits of materialism and dualism, I will point out a more advanced debate where two varieties of materialism are distinguished.

Dualism vs. Materialism

The most famous advocate of mind–body dualism is René Descartes (1596–1650). His view was that every person is composed of (1) a spiritual substance called a soul or a mind, and (2) a physical substance called a body. Seemingly, everything else in the world is physical or spiritual as well. According to Descartes, plants and animals (other than humans) are entirely material, whereas God is spiritual.

Descartes sometimes advocated for dualism on empirical (scientific) grounds. He suspected that reasoning was too complex and subtle an activity to be merely a result of matter sloshing around in your head.

On other occasions, Descartes defended dualism with an a priori argument, which is an argument that does not rely on any appeal to experience or experiment or empirical data but relies solely on logical reasoning. The essence of his argument can arguably be rendered as follows:

1. It is rationally coherent to doubt that you have a body. Just imagine you are a disembodied soul being supplied externally with perceptions that deceive you into thinking you have a body. Although this thought experiment sounds far-fetched, there is nothing contradictory about it.
2. It is not rationally coherent to doubt that you have a mind (or soul). Anyone who entertains the idea that he or she is not a thinking being is *by that very act* guaranteed to be a thinking being. Thus, there is a rational incoherence (or self-refuting quality) to any doubt about the existence of a thinking being.
3. Because the body can be coherently doubted but the mind cannot, they must be different.

This key argument expressed in point 2 is famously abbreviated as "cogito ergo sum" or "I think; therefore I am." It is an intriguing argument worth pondering, but because space is short, we need to move along to one particular deficiency of dualism.

One of the challenges raised by dualism is to explain how certain mental events – our deliberate instigation of physical movement – are able to cause matter to move. Elisabeth of the Palatinate, a.k.a. Princess Elisabeth of Bohemia (1618–80), pressed Descartes to explain

> how the mind of a human being can determine the bodily spirit in producing voluntary actions, being only a thinking substance. For it appears that all determination of movement is produced by the pushing of the thing being moved, by the manner in which it is pushed by that which moves it, or else by the qualification and figure of the surface of the latter. Contact is required for the first two conditions, and extension

> for the third. [But] you entirely exclude the latter from the notion you have of body, and the former seems incompatible with an immaterial thing. (Princess Elisabeth to Descartes, May 6/16, 1643)

In effect, Elisabeth here is using Descartes' own theory of physics against him. If matter is moved only when something external pushes it or when this external source has an appropriate shape, then the causes of motion must contact the matter somewhere or take up space, both of which Descartes denies.

Descartes countered by hypothesizing that the mind moves material bodies through an alternative route of influence – a fundamentally spiritual to physical form of causation – that does not require the mind to take up space or to push matter around through contact forces.

Let's now look retrospectively at the plausibility of a fundamental spiritual to physical causation. Since Descartes' time, our understanding of purely physical causation has progressed enormously, to the point where it appears there are four kinds of fundamental interaction among the various subatomic particles: gravitational, electromagnetic, weak, and strong. Although no one has yet delivered an adequate and complete theory of fundamental physics, it does appear plausible that all interactions among physical bodies are suitable for description in the language of mathematics without needing any mentalistic terminology. There is apparently no behavior we observe among electrons or photons or any other particle, for example, that would be better predicted or explained by positing psionic energy or telekinetic forces or telepathy. What's more, it seems preposterous, given what we now know about how the brain operates, that the action of a subatomic particle could plausibly involve a particle (by itself) thinking or choosing or deliberating or engaging in any mental activity whatsoever. At least, it doesn't seem much more plausible to attribute to an individual electron any sort of fundamental mentality than to assign it fundamental economic or geological attributes. Philosophers have certainly mused about possibilities of this sort, for example (Russell 1927), that molecules can possess a proto-consciousness that emerges as full consciousness when aggregated appropriately as living brains, but there is no theory of how fundamental mental qualities could interact with electrons that even remotely approaches the quality of existing theories of physics. We currently have only the crudest toy theories that emphasize the *possibility* of fundamental mentality interacting with fundamental physicality, not real theories that have succeeded in explaining experimental findings.

The debate between dualism and materialism can now be summarized as follows:

- The dualist believes that the best way to understand mentality is as a fundamental category of existence. Old-fashioned dualists like Descartes say that the soul or mind is a fundamentally different kind of substance than matter, and that claim is known as substance dualism. A modern dualist might brush aside talk of mental *substances* and insist instead that mental *properties* or mental *states* or mental *events* are not fundamentally physical.
- The materialist believes that the best way to understand mentality is as an activity of matter, something that exists just when subatomic particles and fields are appropriately arranged, like in a living brain. The gist of the materialist's conception of mentality is that our talk of the mind is factual only to the extent it expresses facts about the brain. A person might say, "I feel sleepy" instead of "My brain is transitioning to a dormant condition," but according to the materialist, there is nothing to sleepiness beyond the condition of the brain and its broader physical environment.

At present, I have mentioned one argument for materialism over dualism: namely, no one has ever presented a plausible account of how to integrate our rich and experimentally verified theories of physical interaction with any sort of fundamental mentality.

Let us now focus on a second causation-based argument against dualism: the threat of epiphenomenalism. I will define epiphenomenalism, shortly, but we need some stage setting. This second argument starts from the premise that some aspects of mentality, if construed as fundamental, play no plausible role in how matter evolves over time. They might serve as effects but never as causes. Their causal inertness suggests both that they are disposable from our overall account of the world and that we could have no good evidence for their existence. The argument concludes that we should reject any form of dualism that incorporates such forms of fundamental mentality.

The aspect of mentality targeted by this argument is called phenomenality. **Phenomenality** refers to the way our experiences feel to us. Philosophers have several examples that help to convey what phenomenality is. According to a scenario developed by the philosopher Frank Jackson (1986), we imagine a neuroscientist Mary who has been confined her entire life to a monochrome chamber so that she has never seen any colors. For the sake of this example, we are meant to presume that she is capable of seeing and interpreting colors but that she has only been exposed to a gray-scale environment. Mary has studied visual processing so extensively that she knows everything about how humans react to color and the roles that different components of the eyes and brain play in color processing. She knows all the hypothetical relationships like, "If a human with such and such brain condition were to have her eyes exposed to such and such frequencies of light and then asked what color she saw, she would very likely say 'red'." Stated in philosophical jargon, Mary knows all the *functional* aspects of color. Then we imagine Mary leaving the monochrome chamber and seeing colors for the first time. It should hopefully strike you as plausible that Mary would gain some additional understanding of redness by experiencing red for herself. Whatever this experiential understanding amounts to, it is what we call 'phenomenal'. The phenomenal quality of red is how red feels. It is the sensuous quality we experience when we see red objects.

We are now in a position to define **epiphenomenalism** as the doctrine that (1) there exist fundamentally mental states, especially including phenomenal states like "feeling the sensation of a certain shade of red"; (2) these phenomenal states are caused by fundamentally physical states; and (3) these phenomenal states never act as causes. Epiphenomenalism is a special form of dualism, one where causation goes from physical to mental but not in the other direction. According to epiphenomenalism, the spiritual realm is populated with momentary flashes of awareness: phenomenal properties like your present sensation of your visual field that lie together in a temporal sequence but do not influence each other. Because moments of conscious awareness are caused by appropriate brain states, a person whose brain is operating normally will bring about a sequence of these moments of consciousness, and they will seem to be arranged in a stream of consciousness.

Epiphenomalism differs from Descartes' substance dualism by not postulating any immaterial souls that experience the sensations. The main argument for epiphenomenalism over substance dualism is just that epiphenomenalism does not need to solve the difficult task of providing a plausible account of how spiritual properties can influence matter. The epiphenomalist says there is no causation going from the mind to the brain.

If we have accepted the argument so far, that epiphenomenalism is superior to substance dualism, then the final stage for the materialist is to argue that if epiphenomenalism were true, we would have no reason to believe it. The materialist's argument is that if phenomenal states do not have any effect on the brain, then when we are reporting that we have feelings, those reports are being issued by the brain alone, not the phenomenal states that the epiphenomenalist says exist.

So, to summarize the second argument against dualism, the implausibility of spiritual to physical causation should motivate the dualist to adopt epiphenomenalism instead. But epiphenomenalism should also be rejected because it makes it mysterious how we could ever report or react to or have evidence for the world of spirit.

Reductive vs. Non-Reductive Materialism

The materialist world-view is currently very unpopular among the earth's general population. Most people believe in a god or multiple gods or in the existence of other spiritual realms like nirvana or purgatory or heaven. However, materialism is commonly defended by contemporary philosophers who study the mind–body problem. Consequently, much of the academic literature on how the mind fits into a broader meta-physical scheme takes for granted that all mentality is ulti-mately physical. Because philosophers always need to argue about something, materialists tend to fight among themselves about how precisely the physicality of the mind relates to cellular activity in the brain. In particular, they ask, "Should we regard mental activity as somehow *identical* to some kind of brain activity, or are the mind and brain different without violating the materialist doctrine that fundamental reality is ultimately just a bunch of physics?"

The conceptual landscape in this debate is usually charted with two opposing doctrines. The position known as **reduc-tive materialism** claims that mentality is nothing more than physics. The position known as **non-reductive materialism** tries to defend a middle ground in which mentality involves something more than physics, but not in a way that suggests that mentality violates the laws of physics or requires an objectionable addition to the catalogue of physical entities or attributes. I would love to be able to specify the difference between reductive and non-reductive materialism more pre-cisely. Unfortunately, those who engage in this debate define 'reduction' in a variety of ways that obscure the content of the debate.

The reductive materialist often tries to emphasize the pre-sumed *metaphysical* situation: Fundamentally, everything evolves according to laws of physics without any special rules or exceptions that kick in when mentality is involved. Just as there is nothing more to the behavior of a living bacterium than the aggregate behavior of its particles (including its environment), there is nothing more to someone's mental behavior than the aggregate behavior of the particles compos-ing the nervous system and its environment.

The non-reductive materialist often tries to emphasize the presumed *epistemological* situation: It is extremely difficult to draw rich inferences between physics and psychology. One observation non-reductivists often emphasize is that knowing the laws of physics and knowing the catalogue of existing fundamental particles does not allow one to *derive* psychological laws. Another is that mental attributes like cowardice and congeniality cannot be *defined* using only the language of physics. Another observation they make is that psychology is an *autonomous* discipline in the sense that its laws are insulated from the microphysical details about how minds are instantiated. Non-reductivists point out that mentality could plausibly be realized not only in human brains but also in alien life forms and perhaps even in sophisticated computers. This suggests that mental attributes like "being happy" or "understanding algebra" are applicable to beings without nerve cells. Non-reductivists conclude that such mental attributes cannot be identified with neurological attributes like having a certain pattern of neurons firing. In the philosophical jargon, mentality is **multiply realizable**. The non-reductive physicalist concludes from this reasoning that a mental event is not *identical* to the particular way it happens to be physically realized.

One way to mediate the dispute between reductionists and non-reductionists (about mentality) is to point out that there are different ways of thinking about what reduction amounts to. In the metaphysical sense of the term, the reductionist may well be correct that in order to accommodate the existence of mentality, we do not need to supplement or alter our theories of fundamental physics. In the epistemological sense, there are many respects in which facts about physics and facts about psychology are not derivable or explainable or predictable from each other.

Even if the debate can be defused in this way by granting each side its due, we are still left with a project of finding an optimal or at least an auspicious way to describe the relation between mind and body. Let's dig into one further level of detail by tackling a traditional formulation of reductive materialism, the so-called type identity theory, which serves as a traditional foil for non-reductivists.

The **type identity theory** claims that every type of mental state is a type of physical state. The stock example of such a psychophysical identity is the claim that pain is the firing of C fibers. Way back when I was a youngster, grade school textbooks instructed us that C fibers are the kind of nerve tissue that transmit pain signals to the brain. Although no one takes seriously that we feel pain exactly in those cases where C fibers fire, philosophers use "C fibers firing" as a deliberately dumbed-down characterization of whatever neurological activity is felt subjectively as pain. So the advocate for type identity is proposing the equivalence of two types of phenomena: a mental type – pain – and a neurological type whose precise description remains to be found by brain scientists.

The classic advocacy for the type identity theory comes from U. T. Place in "Is Consciousness a Brain Process?" (1956) and Herbert Feigl in "The 'Mental' and the 'Physical'" (1958).[1] Both essays, unfortunately, are aimed less at making a strong case for equating mental types with physical types and more at rebutting potential objections to the identity of mind and brain. Non-reductive materialism can potentially be characterized as a rejection of the type identity theory. According to the non-reductive materialist, all mental activities are realized by some physical process, but a mental activity is not exactly the same as the physical process that realizes it.

Our goal now is to explore how the many theories of causation we have learned apply to the mind–body problem. We will do this by considering three stock arguments that philosophers have formulated.

The Dormativity Argument

In Molière's (1673) *Le Malade Imaginaire*, the character Bachelierus explains why opium puts people to sleep. He says there is a dormative quality in opium whose nature it is to put the senses to sleep.[2] This quip is frequently recited by philosophers to illustrate a form of explanatory failure. It is hardly informative to learn that the reason opium puts people to sleep is that something in opium causes sleepiness. The sort of explanation one normally seeks in such circumstances is a specification of some causal mechanism, an identification of the pertinent chemicals (in terms other than 'whatever it is that causes sleep') together with some story about how these chemicals interact with humans to make them sleep.

The dormativity argument is an argument for adopting reductive physicalism over non-reductive physicalism. In its first step, it attempts to convince us that if materialism is true, then mental events are not "causally efficacious." All the "real causal work" is being done by physical stuff, and mentality is "causally inert." This explanation of how the mental and physical are related parallels the way there are certain active chemicals in opium that cause sleep, and talk of opium's "dormative virtue" is best understood as simply referring to these chemicals, not to something in addition to the chemicals.

In its second step, the dormativity argument presses us to conclude that because mentality is causally inert, we can safely discard it from our list of components of the actual world. According to this reasoning, we should treat mental entities and processes as non-fundamental. They do not constitute anything extra in the world beyond the physical stuff in our brains and the brain's broader environment. This conclusion is essentially reductive physicalism: The actual world contains no mental entities or processes *in addition to* physical stuff.

The Qua Problem

A closely related problem concerns the "causal efficacy" of mental properties. The Latin term 'qua' has been adopted in philosophy to designate a focus on a particular property or role. You can often translate 'qua' as 'insofar as it is a'. For example, when a ham is being used to prop open a door, the solidity and weight of the ham play a role in causing the door to remain open whereas its nutritional content is not causally relevant. Accordingly, we say, "The ham *qua food* does not prevent the door from closing, but the ham *qua solid heavy object* does serve as an effective doorstop."

The qua problem for mental causation is the task of ensuring that one's proposed solution to the mind–body problem permits a mental entity to engage in causation *qua mental entity*. Non-reductive materialists agree that all mental events are physically realized, but it is unclear whether the *mentality* of the mental events plays a role in causation or whether it is only the *physicality* of the mental event that engages in causation.

If a non-reductivist's proposed resolution of the mind–body problem can be shown to involve only the physical aspects of the mental event in mental causation, then the theory can be accused of not vindicating the claim that our mental aspects are capable of (and routinely do) cause effects qua mental aspects.

The Causal Exclusion Argument

Another argument against non-reductive materialism is the causal exclusion argument, which attempts to establish the inefficacy of (the non-reductive materialist's proposed) mental entities by showing that they "have no causal work to do." The argument starts from the proposition that physical events provide a complete causal explanation for any physical event without needing to invoke anything mental. If mental causes are also causally efficacious, then rampant causal overdetermination would exist. There would be many physical events with two distinct causes at the same time: a physical cause and a mental cause. Such overdetermination is thought to be problematic because it would imply that nature incorporates an unacceptable causal redundancy. The completeness of physical causation excludes the mental from doing any *non-redundant* causal work, and that provides an opportunity and motivation to adopt a more austere conception of the actual world that leaves out these "extra" mental properties.

Summary

Let's now review the case against non-reductive materialism before considering how a non-reductive materialist might fend off the attacks.

The three tenets that constitute non-reductive materialism can be characterized as follows:

First, the properties studied in psychology are not identical to physical properties, since they are multiply realized by them.

Second, mental properties nevertheless supervene on physical properties in the sense that there cannot be a difference with respect to mental properties without a further difference with respect to physical properties. Third, mental properties are causes and effects of other properties.[3]

The three arguments in the preceding section in effect contend that the first and third principles conflict. To the extent mental properties count as entities in addition to the physics, these "additional entities" have poor credentials as causes. All three arguments try to persuade us that if the "higher-level" properties of psychology are not identical to whatever fundamental physical properties instantiate mentality, then we can dismiss their existence as causative agents in the actual world.

One further observation to keep in mind is that the structure of this argument matches the "threat of epiphenomenalism" argument against dualism. Recall the two parts of that argument: First, from the implausibility of any fundamental spiritual to physical causation, it concludes that the dualist's proposed mind cannot cause physical effects. Second, it points out that if the dualist's proposed mind does not cause physical effects, we cannot gather any evidence for its existence. The reductive materialist is saying much the same about the non-reductivist's proposed conception of mentality. Whatever this extra entity is that goes beyond the physical presence of the mind, it does not engage in causation. Consequently, we do not have any of the normal causation-based evidence for it.

Not every reductivist argument against non-reductive materialism goes exactly like the one I have presented, but it should capture the gist of the reductivist's overall position. Remember that 'reduction' is such a contested concept that it is hard to pin down what precisely the disagreement is about.

Non-Reductive vs. Reductive Materialism

To defend non-reductive materialism from these reductivist attacks, several lines of reasoning have been developed.

One option is to claim that fundamental physics does not provide a comprehensive account of how nature evolves (O'Connor and Wong 2005). The operative hypothesis here is that there are special rules governing matter when it is organized as a brain so that the electrons and quarks that engage in neural activity are not causally the same as ordinary arrangements of electrons and quarks. In the technical jargon, mental properties are "emergent," which means they are instantiated by ordinary matter, but that the matter does not behave in the default manner described by physics. (The commonest response to this option is to point out that although emergence is possible, no one has ever demonstrated a violation of the existing theories of physics that would suggest it is a plausible hypothesis. Also, be aware that the term 'emergent' suffers from just as much ambiguity as 'reduction'.)

Another tactic is to deny that mental entities are causally nothing more than their physical realizers (Wilson 2011). One way of cashing out this idea says that mental states have causal powers that are not identical with their physical realizers because the physical realizers can do more than just mental activity. The customer's desire to leave the store includes the power to activate his limbs but does not include the power (possessed by the brain) to transport potassium across cellular membranes. The operative strategy here is to organize the entities and properties of psychology into hierarchies based on their associated powers. These powers-based distinctions, the argument goes, are robust enough to vindicate the non-reductivist's claim that mental states are not identical with certain physical states. (The most plausible reductivist response is to argue that this option is billed by its advocates as non-reductive, but it is actually compatible with a reductivist interpretation, so that the disagreement is largely an issue of rhetorical emphasis and terminology.)

Another option is to argue that a difference-making conception of causation avoids the kinds of commitments needed for the success of the dormativity argument, the qua argument, and the causal exclusion argument (Loewer 2002). If causation is merely counterfactual dependence, for example, then the unreduced psychological entity or property does make a bona fide causal difference. The customer's desire for a lower price caused him to leave the store. How is that? If the customer had not had a desire for a lower price, then his brain would have been in a different configuration, one that would not have sent signals to his legs to exit the store. (The commonest response to this option is to recite the kinds of problems that generally face difference-making accounts of causation.)

A variant of this strategy has been developed for interventionist theories of causation as well (Menzies 2008; Raatikainen 2010) The basic idea is that one can develop one causal model representing the relationships between psychological variables and another causal model representing the relationships between physical variables, and if so, a happy coexistence can be achieved. The interventionist conception does not dictate that there be a uniquely correct model for every case of causation.

In chapter 1, I suggested that it is convenient to distinguish between productive and difference-making conceptions of causation. We have already seen that counterfactual theories of causation might make sense of the causal relevance of mental properties assuming that the physical automatically gives rise to the mental. The answer is that if your mental state were different, your physical state would have to be different and that would give rise to physical effects in the future. But can counterfactual theories succeed without incorporating aspects of production? If they cannot, do the problems of mental causation again press against non-reductive materialism?

Summary

It is important not to get too lost in all the details, so let's review the main points. Mental causation is a problem case for anyone who thinks the actual world contains more than just fundamental physics operating in its ordinary way. This is simply the problem of developing a plausible scheme under which the extra stuff – the mind, the soul, beliefs, willpower, whatever – can exist as components or aspects of the actual world while peacefully contributing to the causal development of material substances.

The hard part to settle is the scientific question, which is, "Does physics in principle provide an empirically adequate account of all observable interactions?" One might believe that physics alone could never predict a certain beggar's whimsical decision to break into song. One might believe that it is only human hubris that supports the hypothesis that people have souls that redirect the atoms in their brains. It is hard to settle this question without comprehensive scientific evidence.

The easy part to settle arises only among people who believe that the predictive ideal can be achieved solely with physics. This is the philosophical question, "How should we organize our concepts to best characterize the relation between mental and physical?" Much of the debate at this stage consists of wrangling over what makes something counts as a *real addition* to the ideal physics rather than just an *additional name* for aspects of the ideal physics.

Questions

Q: What do we need to know about causation?

A: Because you can review all of the material without me, let me try to impart some summary judgments about the place of causation in the general scheme of things. I'll break this topic up to address three audiences.

First, for anyone interested in causation from a philosophical angle – in particular a metaphysics of causation – I think great progress can be made in exploring how best to think of causation and its relation to fundamental reality. That is what I have tried to do in my career, and I do not see any reason to be discouraged despite decades of philosophical stagnation.

Second, for anyone interested in causation from a scientific perspective, trying to figure out what causes what, whether it be in ecology or planetary science, I think the general resources like the principles of causal modeling and the specific techniques employed by each discipline are reasonable guides to follow. However, I do think that if you embark on a scientific career, you would do well to be mindful of the large variety of pitfalls that make causal inferences treacherous. For example, some of the statistical tools used in sciences where data is expensive to gather, like medical science, are conceptually suspect and frequently misunderstood even by leading experts. And the institutional structure of science leads to bias in ways that have been publicly recognized but not adequately addressed. For all its shortcomings, science in its current form is still far superior (in intellectual rigor and trustworthiness) to other institutions like private business, governments, militaries, and religion, but science has room for improvement too. Scientific use of the concept of causality, for example, is still embarrassingly imprecise even though science gets along fairly well without being clear about its causal notions. Maybe you can help to improve conceptual hygiene in your future workplace.

Third, for anyone interested in causation from a moral or legal perspective, the situation is less sanguine, in my opinion. Sound judgments about singular causation, including those that are thought to be intuitively obvious, are frequently incoherent when collected together. And I doubt that there is any tractable way to make them rigorously consistent. A brief examination of our attitudes about imposing risks on one another might help to illustrate my suspicion.

Consider how the legal system in most jurisdictions imposes punishment on people who cause injury to someone else in the presence of some identifiable factor that promotes the injury. For example, if someone drives an automobile into a pedestrian while intoxicated or legally blind or watching a movie, we tend to judge that the driver caused the injury and deserves some sanction. What justifies the punishment? There is a lot to be said, but one plausible principle is that it is wrong to impose too high of a risk of injury on other people without some outstanding potential gain to be achieved. Knowing that he is distracted or impaired, the driver is choosing to significantly increase the chance of harming others for his own small gain of saving some travel time.

Digging into further details, how are we to measure risk? To some extent, we care about the absolute magnitude of the risk imposed on others, and to some extent, we care about the relative magnitude. Driving while just barely legally drunk, for example, multiplies one's risk of killing someone on average by about a factor of seven, on average. This imposition of extra risk on others is normally judged as immoral even though the chance of killing another person during a one-mile drive is so low that it is not morally noteworthy.

If we take the correctness of this moral judgment for granted, our judgments about the following scenario might be puzzling. Suppose I have chosen to dine at a restaurant seven miles away rather than at a restaurant one mile away because the meals are generally tastier. I have in effect imposed a seven-times higher risk on other people by driving to the distant restaurant in exchange for the small gain to myself of tastier food. And I have imposed about the same absolute level of risk on others as a drunk who drove one mile. Most people, when asked about this second scenario, do not think that there is anything immoral about my choice to drive to the distant restaurant.

Now ask yourself, "Why should there be any significant difference between our moral judgments in these two cases?" Why are drunk drivers stigmatized while drivers who travel further than necessary get a free pass to impose as much risk on others as their gas money allows?

I am not going to try to justify the difference in people's attitudes toward these two cases because I do not think there is a good justification, but I would like to point out that after a traffic accident has occurred, it is usually much easier for authorities to identify a driver as drunk than to identify a driver who was driving for too frivolous a reason. At least, authorities do not want to take up the task of evaluating whether each driver's reason for being on the road is good enough to outweigh the increased risk they are imposing on others.

To apply this discussion back to causation, consider that we tend to judge that being drunk was one of the major contributing factors to the drunk driver's accident, but we probably do not judge that being sober but wanting to eat at a better restaurant was a major contributing factor to an otherwise similar accident. This demonstrates not only that our causal judgments do not match up to what we ought to care about if we wanted to adopt a more judicious approach to imposing risks on others. I think it also illustrates that we do not have morally neutral assessments of causation that we then employ in our moral judgments. Quite to the contrary, our beliefs about what is impermissible or mandatory play a role in how we select (among the numerous contributing causes) those causes deserving special emphasis. Finally, this illustrates that practical problems regarding enforcement play a role in what we think causes what. Ideally, we should treat the two discussed causes of increased risk the same. The excessive alcohol consumption caused the one injury, and the unwarranted length of the other trip caused the other injury, and both did so by increasing the probability that someone would be injured by the same amount. Yet, because there is no practical way to enforce a general rule against imposing seven times the usual automobile-related risks on other people, we ignore the kinds of causes that are hard to adjudicate, even if they are significantly worse in terms of objective risk than driving while intoxicated.

If you are interested, you can find some evidence for these claims in some of the psychological literature on causal judgment. My overall point is simply that our judgments about singular causation are a jumble of sometimes conflicting rules of thumb, and I do not think we will ever find any comprehensive, adequate, and tractable rule of the form, "c is a cause of e if and only if. . . ." It would be much better to drop the pretense that if we could just navigate past two or three counterexamples to our existing accounts, there would be clear sailing ahead.

Notes

1 Introduction: All Things Causal

1 The quotation is from the first paragraph of Sellars (1962).
2 Introduced by Hall (2004).
3 Rhinoceroses, oryxes, and other creatures were sometimes classified as unicorns and they exist today, but I have in mind the more delicate equine unicorns with the long straight horn. You should read about the history of unicorns. It's fun.
4 Perhaps 'potential cause' is meant to clarify the view that talk of type causation is more accurately described as talk about possible relations of causation that hold by virtue of causal generalities in the actual world, like how unicorns (by their nature) have the potential to cause hoof-marks because of how hoofed animals in general interact with mud.
5 For example, Hugh Mellor (1995, p. 7) declares, "Smoking causes cancer . . . if and only if smokers' cancers are generally caused by their smoking." Another example appears in Lewis (1973a, p. 558): "A sentence of the form 'C-events cause E-events,' for instance, can mean any of (a) For some c in C and some e in E, c causes e. (b) For every e in E, there is some c in C such that c causes e. (c) For every c in C, there is some e in E such that c causes e."
6 Locke (1690, ch. 5 sec. 27): "Though the earth, and all inferior creatures, be common to all men, yet every man has a property in his own person: this no body has any right to but himself. The labour of his body, and the work of his hands, we may say, are properly his. Whatsoever then he removes out of the state

that nature hath provided, and left it in, he hath mixed his labour with, and joined to it something that is his own, and thereby makes it his property. It being by him removed from the common state nature hath placed it in, it hath by this labour something annexed to it, that excludes the common right of other men: for this labour being the unquestionable property of the labourer, no man but he can have a right to what that is once joined to, at least where there is enough, and as good, left in common for others."

2 Causal Oomph

1 I have deliberately inserted a bad argument here. See if you can find out what is wrong with it.

3 Process and Mechanism

1 See also Dowe (2009).
2 See Salmon (1984, pp. 196–202); Dowe (2000, sec. II. 6); Williamson (2005, sec. 7.3, 2009, p. 201).
3 See Railton (1978) for an earlier discussion.

4 Difference-Making

1 Previously, I distinguished between narrowly and broadly defined causes, and that distinction is largely the same as between very fragile and not-so-fragile events.
2 Slote (1978, p. 26, footnote 33).
3 See especially Hitchcock (1996).

6 Probability-Raising

1 These are the Kolmogorov axioms.
2 Also, the actual pattern of die roll outcomes satisfies other statistical measures that indicate "probabilistic independence," which is intuitively that taking into account the outcome of one die roll does not help one predict other die roll outcomes.
3 Reichenbach (1935). See also Glymour and Eberhardt (2012).
4 See Hitchcock (2012).

7 Manipulation and Intervention

1 See also Halpern and Pearl (2001, 2005); Hall (2007); Halpern (2008); Hitchcock (2009a); Halpern and Hitchcock (2010).

8 Mental Causation

1 See also Carnap (1932, p. 127); Reichenbach (1938); and Schlick (1935).
2 "Quia est in eo / Virtus dormitiva, / Cujus est natura / Sensus assoupire."
3 Slightly adapted from List and Menzies (2008, p. 1).

Bibliography

Arntzenius, F. (1990). "Physics and Common Causes," *Synthese* 82, 77–96.

Aronson, J. (1979). "On the Grammar of 'Cause'," *Synthese* 22, 414–30.

Beebee, H. (2004). "Causing and Nothingness," in J. Collins, N. Hall, and L. A. Paul (eds.), *Causation and Counterfactuals*. Cambridge: MIT Press.

Beebee, H. (2006). *Hume on Causation*. New York: Routledge.

Beebee, H., Hitchcock, C., and Menzies, P., eds. (2009). *The Oxford Handbook of Causation*. Oxford: Oxford University Press.

Bickel, P. J., Hammel, E. A., and O'Connell, J. W. (1975). "Sex Bias in Graduate Admissions: Data from Berkeley," *Science* 187 (4175), 398–404.

Carnap, R. (1932). "Psychologie in Physikalischer Sprache," *Erkenntnis* 3, 107–42. Translated in A. J. Ayer (ed.), *Logical Positivism*. Glencoe, IL: Free Press, 1959.

Cartwright, N. (1979). "Causal Laws and Effective Strategies," *Noûs* 13, 419–37. Reprinted in N. Cartwright, *How the Laws of Physics Lie*. Oxford: Clarendon Press, 1983.

Craver, C. (2005). "Beyond Reduction: Mechanisms and Multifield Integration and the Unity of Neuroscience," *Studies in History and Philosophy of Science Part C: Studies in History and Philosophy of Biological and Biomedical Sciences* 36 (2), 373–95.

Craver, C. (2007). *Explaining the Brain*. New York: Oxford University Press.

Davidson, D. (1967). "Causal Relations," *Journal of Philosophy* 64, 691–703.

Dowe, P. (2000). *Physical Causation*. Cambridge: Cambridge University Press.

Dowe, P. (2009). "Causal Process Theories," in H. Beebee, C. Hitchcock, and P. Menzies (eds.), *The Oxford Handbook of Causation*. Oxford: Oxford University Press.

Dummett, M. (1964). "Bringing about the Past," *Philosophical Review* 73 (3), 338–59.

Edgington, D. (1995). "On Conditionals," *Mind* 104 (414), 235–329.

Eells, E. (1991). *Probabilistic Causality*. Cambridge: Cambridge University Press.

Fair, D. (1979). "Causation and the Flow of Energy," *Erkenntnis* 14, 219–50.

Feigl, H. (1958). "The 'Mental' and the 'Physical'," in H. Feigl, M. Scriven, and G. Maxwell (eds.), *Concepts, Theories and the Mind–Body Problem*. Minneapolis: University of Minneapolis Press.

Garrett, D. (2009). "Hume," in H. Beebee, C. Hitchcock, and P. Menzies (eds.), *The Oxford Handbook of Causation*. Oxford: Oxford University Press.

Glennan, S. (1996). "Mechanisms and the Nature of Causation," *Erkenntnis* 44 (1), 49–71.

Glennan, S. (2009). "Mechanisms," in H. Beebee, C. Hitchcock, and P. Menzies (eds.), *The Oxford Handbook of Causation*. Oxford: Oxford University Press.

Glymour, C. and Eberhardt, F. (2012). "Hans Reichenbach," in E. N. Zalta (ed.), *The Stanford Encyclopedia of Philosophy* (Winter 2012 Edition), http://plato.stanford.edu/archives/win2012/entries/reichenbach.

Good, I. J. (1961). "A Causal Calculus I," *British Journal for the Philosophy of Science* 11, 305–18.

Good, I. J. (1962). "A Causal Calculus II," *British Journal for the Philosophy of Science* 12, 43–51.

Goodman, N. (1947). "The Problem of Counterfactual Conditionals," *Journal of Philosophy* 44, 113–28.

Hall, N. (2000). "Causation and the Price of Transitivity," *Journal of Philosophy* 97, 198–222.

Hall, N. (2004). "Two Concepts of Causation," in J. Collins, N. Hall, and L. A. Paul (eds.), *Causation and Counterfactuals*. Cambridge: MIT Press.

Hall, N. (2007). "Structural Equations and Causation," *Philosophical Studies* 132, 109–36.

Halpern, J. Y. (2008). "Defaults and Normality in Causal Structures," http://arxiv.org/abs/0806.2140.

Halpern, J. Y. and Hitchcock, C. (2010). "Actual Causation and the Art of Modeling," in R. Dechter, H. Geffner, and J. Y. Halpern (eds.), *Heuristics, Probability and Causality: A Tribute to Judea Pearl*. London: College Publications.

Halpern, J. Y. and Pearl, J. (2001). "Causes and Explanations: A Structural-Model Approach – Part I: Causes," in *Proceedings of the Seventeenth Conference on Uncertainty in Artificial Intelligence (UAI 2001)*. San Francisco, CA: Morgan Kaufmann, 194–202.

Halpern, J. Y. and Pearl, J. (2005). "Causes and Explanations: A Structural-Model Approach – Part II: Explanations," *British Journal for Philosophy of Science* 56 (4), 843–87.

Hesslow, G. (1981). "Causality and Determinism," *Philosophy of Science* 48, 591–605.

Hitchcock, C. (1995). "Salmon on Explanatory Relevance," *Philosophy of Science* 62, 304–20.

Hitchcock, C. (1996). "The Role of Contrast in Causal and Explanatory Claims," *Synthese* 107 (3), 395–419.

Hitchcock, C. (2009a). "Structural Equations and Causation: Six Counterexamples," *Philosophical Studies* 144, 391–401.

Hitchcock, C. (2009b). "Causal Modelling," in H. Beebee, C. Hitchcock, and P. Menzies (eds.), *The Oxford Handbook of Causation*. Oxford: Oxford University Press.

Hitchcock, C. (2012). "Probabilistic Causation," in E. N. Zalta (ed.), *The Stanford Encyclopedia of Philosophy* (Winter 2012 Edition), http://plato.stanford.edu/archives/win2012/entries/causation-probabilistic.

Hume, D. (1739). *A Treatise of Human Nature*. London.

Hume, D. (1748). *An Enquiry Concerning Human Understanding*. London.

Jackson, F. (1986). "What Mary Didn't Know," *Journal of Philosophy* 83 (5), 291–5.

James, W. (1897). "The Dilemma of Determinism," in W. James, *The Will to Believe and Other Essays in Popular Philosophy*. Cambridge: John Wilson and Son.

Kistler, M. (1999). *Causalité et Lois de la Nature*. Paris: Vrin. Translated as *Causality and Laws of Nature*. New York: Routledge, 2006.

Kutach, D. (2013). *Causation and Its Basis in Fundamental Physics*. New York: Oxford University Press.

Kvart, I. (1986). *A Theory of Counterfactuals*. Indianapolis: Hackett.

Laplace, P. (1820). *Essai Philosophique sur les Probabilités*, in P. Laplace, *Théorie Analytique des Probabilités*. Paris: V. Courcier. Translated in F. W. Truscott and F. L. Emory (trans.), *A Philosophical Essay on Probabilities*. New York: Dover, 1951.

Lewis, D. (1973a). "Causation," *Journal of Philosophy* 70, 556–67. Reprinted in D. Lewis, *Philosophical Papers*. Vol. 2. Oxford: Oxford University Press, 1986.

Lewis, D. (1973b). *Counterfactuals*. Oxford: Blackwell.

List, C. and Menzies, P. (2008). "Non-Reductive Physicalism and the Limits of the Exclusion Principle," http://philsci-archive.pitt.edu/id/eprint/4322.

Locke, J. (1690). *Second Treatise of Government*. London.

Loewer, B. (2002). "Comments on Jaegwon Kim's *Mind in a Physical World*," *Philosophy and Phenomenological Research* 65 (3), 655–62.

Mach, E. (1883). *Die Mechanik in ihrer Entwickelung*. Leipzig: F. A. Brockhaus. Translated in T. J. McCormack (trans.) *The Science of Mechanics: A Critical and Historical Account of its Development*. La Salle, IL: Open Court, 1943.

Machamer, P., Darden, L., and Craver, C. (2000). "Thinking about Mechanisms," *Philosophy of Science* 67 (1), 1–25.

Mackie, J. L. (1973). *The Cement of the Universe*. Oxford: Oxford University Press.

Maslen, C. (2004). "Causes, Contrasts, and the Nontransitivity of Causation," in J. Collins, N. Hall, and L. A. Paul (eds.), *Causation and Counterfactuals*. Cambridge: MIT Press.

McGrath, S. (2005). "Causation by Omission: A Dilemma," *Philosophical Studies* 123, 125–49.

McLaughlin, J. A. (1925). "Proximate Cause," *Harvard Law Review* 39 (2), 149–99.

Mellor, H. (1995). *The Facts of Causation*. New York: Routledge.

Menzies, P. (2008). "The Exclusion Problem, the Determination Relation, and Contrastive Causation," in J. Hohwy and J. Kallestrup (eds.), *Being Reduced: New Essays on Reduction, Explanation and Causation*. Oxford: Oxford University Press.

Menzies, P. and Price, H. (1993). "Causation as a Secondary Quality," *British Journal for the Philosophy of Science* 44, 187–203.

Mill, J. S. (1930 [1843]). *A System of Logic: Ratiocinative and Inductive*. London: Longmans, Green.

Molière (Jean-Baptiste Poquelin) (1673). *Le Malade Imaginaire*.

Ney, A. (2009). "Physical Causation and Difference-Making," *British Journal for the Philosophy of Science* 60 (4), 737–64.

Norton, J. (2008). "The Dome: An Unexpectedly Simple Failure of Determinism," *Philosophy of Science* 75, 786–98.

O'Connor, T. and Wong, H. Y. (2005). "The Metaphysics of Emergence," *Noûs* 39 (4), 658–78.

Paul, L. A. (2009). "Counterfactual Theories," in H. Beebee, C. Hitchcock, and P. Menzies (eds.), *The Oxford Handbook of Causation.* Oxford: Oxford University Press.

Pearl, J. (2000). *Causality: Models, Reasoning, and Inference.* Cambridge: Cambridge University Press.

Place, U. T. (1956). "Is Consciousness a Brain Process?" *British Journal of Psychology* 47 (1), 44–50.

Price, H. (forthcoming). "Causation, Intervention, and Agency: Woodward on Menzies and Price," in H. Beebee, C. Hitchcock, and H. Price (eds.), *Making a Difference.* Oxford: Oxford University Press.

Psillos, S. (2009). "Regularity Theories," in H. Beebee, C. Hitchcock, and P. Menzies (eds.), *The Oxford Handbook of Causation.* Oxford: Oxford University Press.

Raatikainen, P. (2010). "Causation, Exclusion, and the Special Sciences," *Erkenntnis* 73, 349–63.

Railton, P. (1978). "A Deductive-Nomological Model of Probabilistic Explanation," *Philosophy of Science* 45, 206–26.

Reichenbach, H. (1935). *Wahrscheinlichkeitslehre: Eine Untersuchung über die Logischen und Mathematischen Grundlagen der Wahrscheinlichkeitsrechnung.* Leiden: Sijthoff. Revised as E. H. Hutten and H. Reichenbach (trans.), *The Theory of Probability: An Inquiry into the Logical and Mathematical Foundations of the Calculus of Probability.* Berkeley: University of California Press, 1949.

Reichenbach, H. (1938). *Experience and Prediction.* Chicago: University of Chicago Press.

Reichenbach, H. (1956). *The Direction of Time.* Berkeley: University of California Press.

Russell, B. (1913). "On the Notion of Cause," *Proceedings of the Aristotelian Society* 13, 1–26.

Russell, B. (1927). *The Analysis of Matter.* London: Routledge.

Salmon, W. (1984). *Scientific Explanation and the Causal Structure of the World.* Princeton: Princeton University Press.

Salmon, W. (1993). "Causality: Production and Propagation," in E. Sosa and M. Tooley (eds.), *Causation.* Oxford: Oxford University Press.

Salmon, W. (1997). "Causality and Explanation: A Reply to Two Critiques," *Philosophy of Science* 64, 461–77.

Schaffer, J. (2000). "Overlappings: Probability-Raising without Causation," *Australasian Journal of Philosophy* 78, 40–46.

Schlick, M. (1935). "De la Relation des Notions Psychologiques et des Notions Physiques," *Revue de Synthèse* 10, 5–26. Translated in H. Feigl and W. Sellars (eds.) *Readings in Philosophical Analysis*. New York: Appleton-Century Crofts, 1949.

Sellars, W. (1962). "Philosophy and the Scientific Image of Man," in R. Colodny (ed.), *Frontiers of Science and Philosophy*. Pittsburgh: University of Pittsburgh Press. Reprinted in W. Sellars, *Science, Perception and Reality*. London: Routledge & Kegan Paul, 1963.

Shepherd, M. (1824). *An Essay upon the Relation of Cause and Effect*. London: Hookman.

Simpson, E. (1951). "The Interpretation of Interaction in Contingency Tables," *Journal of the Royal Statistical Society, Ser. B* 13 (2), 238–41.

Slote, M. (1978). "Time in Counterfactuals," *Philosophical Review* 87, 3–27.

Sober, E. (2001). "Venetian Sea Levels, British Bread Prices, and the Principle of the Common Cause," *British Journal for the Philosophy of Science* 52 (2), 311–46.

Spirtes, P., Glymour, C., and Scheines, R. (2000). *Causation, Prediction, and Search*. Cambridge: MIT Press.

Strevens, M. (2007). "Mackie Remixed," in J. Keim Campbell, M. O'Rourke, and H. S. Silverstein (eds.), *Causation and Explanation*. Cambridge: MIT Press.

Suppes, P. (1970). *A Probabilistic Theory of Causality*. Amsterdam: North-Holland.

Venn, J. (1866). *The Logic of Chance*. London: Macmillan.

Williamson, J. (2005). *Bayesian Nets and Causality*. Oxford: Oxford University Press.

Williamson, J. (2009). "Probabilistic Theories," in H. Beebee, C. Hitchcock, and P. Menzies (eds.), *The Oxford Handbook of Causation*. Oxford: Oxford University Press.

Wilson, J. (2011). "Non-Reductive Realization and the Powers-Based Subset Strategy," *Monist*, 94 (1), 121–54.

Woodward, J. (2003). *Making Things Happen: A Theory of Causal Explanation*. Oxford: Oxford University Press.

Woodward, J. (2009). "Agency and Interventionist Theories," in H. Beebee, C. Hitchcock, and P. Menzies (eds.), *The Oxford Handbook of Causation*. Oxford: Oxford University Press.

Woodward, J. (2012). "Causation and Manipulability", in E. N. Zalta (ed.), *The Stanford Encyclopedia of Philosophy* (Winter 2012 Edition), http://plato.stanford.edu/archives/win2012/entries/causation-mani.

von Wright, G. H. (1971a). "On the Logic and Epistemology of the Causal Relation," in P. Suppes, L. Henkin, G. C. Moisil, and

A. Joja (eds.), *Logic, Methodology, and Philosophy of Science IV*. Amsterdam: North-Holland.

von Wright, G. H. (1971b). *Explanation and Understanding*. Ithaca, NY: Cornell University Press.

von Wright, G. H. (1974). *Causality and Determinism*. New York: Columbia University Press.

Index